shaping tomorrow with you

Introduction to Carrier Ethernet
for Carrier Ethernet Professionals

Second Edition - November 2015

Fujitsu Network Communications Inc.

https://partners.fnc.fujitsu.com

ISBN 10: 15 9117566

ISBN 13: 978-1519117564

Fujitsu welcomes your feedback and suggestions for this book or future Carrier Ethernet educational material. Please use the email address below for all feedback.

For comments or questions, contact us at ReaderFeedback@fnc.fujitsu.com.

Contents

1

Introduction

In this chapter:

1.1   Preface
1.2   What is Carrier Ethernet?

This book is an entry-level introduction to Carrier Ethernet, intended for anyone new to Carrier Ethernet, including those with little or no background in computer networking and/or telecommunications. It has two aims: (1) to explain networking technology leading up to and motivating Carrier Ethernet and (2) to explain Carrier Ethernet conceptually within this framework. This book was conceived to be a prequel to Fujitsu's MEF-CECP Study Guide (any edition), but can be used alone (as an introduction to Carrier Ethernet) or in combination with other professional certification training materials.

Carrier Ethernet emerges in the overlap between two highly evolved realms of commercial networking technology: (1) enterprise[1] computer networking and (2) telecommunications networking. At one time these realms were very distinct, but for some years now they have been evolving toward convergence. Many professionals interested in Carrier Ethernet lack fundamental knowledge in one or both realms, as well as a clear framework for understanding their convergence and Carrier Ethernet's place in the evolution.

Training resources for Carrier Ethernet professional certification tend to assume significant background knowledge and focus on mastering the details needed to pass an exam over core fundamentals and motivations. This book is designed to complement such material, focusing instead on explaining the big picture, the core background technologies, the context, the motivations, and the concepts that underpin Carrier Ethernet. The main goal is to impart a strong foundation for understanding Carrier Ethernet in a general sense. A secondary goal is to offer insights into the evolution of networking technology and the issues that surround and motivate Carrier Ethernet.

Chapter 1 provides a synopsis of the book and a brief explanation of Carrier Ethernet. Chapter 2 explains Ethernet in local area networking, starting from first principles and simple contexts and gradually building up to include MAC bridging and VLAN bridging. Chapter 3 describes traditional Telecom technology and wide area networking solutions prior to Carrier Ethernet. Chapter 4 provides a high-level overview of Carrier Ethernet. The appendix includes supportive details related to various of topics covered in the book.

---

1   **Enterprise**– Any organization, such as a business, a non-profit, a university, or a government agency.

1.1
Preface

Knowledge about Carrier Ethernet is in demand, especially among the wide variety of professionals involved in buying, selling, providing or using carrier services or equipment. The MEF awards anyone who demonstrates knowledge of Carrier Ethernet (by passing an exam) accreditation as an MEF Carrier Ethernet Certified Professional (MEF-CECP). To prepare for the MEF-CECP exam, many people take an MEF-CECP exam training course or study on their own using an MEF-CECP exam study guide. However, these training resources typically assume prior knowledge of computer and Telecom networking that many people do not have.

This book is designed to help technically savvy people quickly acquire the prerequisite knowledge they need to make efficient use of MEF-CECP exam training classes and/or study materials. It was conceived to be a companion to Fujitsu's MEF-CECP Study Guide (any edition), but can be used alone (as an introduction to Carrier Ethernet) or in combination with other Carrier Ethernet training materials.

Assuming little or no prior understanding of Ethernet, local area networking, wide area networking, or telecommunications, this book builds the knowledge base needed to understand Carrier Ethernet and related technology well enough to begin training specifically for the MEF-CECP exam.

Regarding This 2nd Edition

The first edition of this book was titled *Introduction to Carrier Ethernet: A foundation for MEF-CECP 2.0 training*. In this second edition, *2.0* has been removed from the subtitle because the MEF no longer recognizes MEF-CECP 2.0 certification.[2] This change in title is the main reason for publishing this second edition. Material in the first edition was not out of date, but the title gave the impression that it was out of date, so it needed to change. Additionally, the opportunity was taken to review content and improve it where possible. Improvements include the removal of peripheral reference material from the appendix, minor revisions to Chapter 4 and the clean up of minor issues throughout the book.

About the Authors

Jon Kieffer (MEF-CECP) is a principal technical writer working for Fujitsu Network Communications since 2001. Previous to that, Jon taught software engineering at the University of Hull, U.K., and mechanical engineering at the Australian National University. Jon holds BS, MS, and PhD degrees in mechanical engineering and has authored 12 refereed journal articles and more than 30 conference papers in the fields of mechanical and controls engineering. The MEF has recognized Jon as an outstanding contributor for contributions to the MEF-CECP program in 2013, 2014 and 2015. In 2015, Jon received the MEF Marketing Committee Editors Award for co-editing the MEF white paper Understanding Bandwidth Profiles in MEF 6.2 Service Definitions.

Yongchao Fan (CCIE R&S #6369) is a product support engineer working for Fujitsu Network Communications since 1999 and previously worked for IBM as a global services engineer. Yongchao holds BS and MS degrees in computer science and has extensive experience with various networking technologies and real-world networks.

Reader Feedback — Fujitsu welcomes your feedback and suggestions for this book or future Carrier Ethernet educational material. If you have comments or questions, please contact us at **ReaderFeedback@fnc.fujitsu.com**.

---

2 In April 2015, the MEF announced an expiration policy for professional certification and unified prior certifications, MEF-CECP and MEF-CECP 2.0, into one certification, called the MEF-CECP.

1.2
What is Carrier Ethernet?

In this section:

1.2.1   Carrier Ethernet in a Nutshell
1.2.2   Elements of the Carrier Ethernet Services
1.2.3   Example Carrier Ethernet Service Applications

A **carrier** is a service provider such as AT&T, T-Mobile, Verizon, Comcast, Sprint, or Time Warner Cable that provides voice and/or data services to customers spread over large geographic areas. Carrier networking grew out of Telecom networking and basically rebrands the industry to emphasize newer data services over older circuit services (the foundation of traditional voice-based telecommunications). The vast majority of traffic in carrier networks is now data traffic, and carrier networking technology has been evolving since the 1980s to support it more efficiently.

Carrier Ethernet is a major initiative within the industry to redefine services for the full spectrum of carrier applications based on standardized technology-agnostic service definitions with Ethernet used as the standard interface for all services.

The **MEF**, or **MEF Forum**[3], is a nonprofit global industry alliance and the defining body for Carrier Ethernet comprising more than 220 organizations, including carriers, cable MSOs (Multiple Service Operators), network equipment/software manufacturers, semiconductor vendors, and testing organizations. The MEF develops Carrier Ethernet technical specifications and implementation agreements to promote interoperability and the deployment of Carrier Ethernet networks and services worldwide. The MEF web site is mef.net/.

1.2.1
Carrier Ethernet in a Nutshell

Carrier Ethernet is defined by MEF standards that address a wide variety of issues. However, the unifying purpose of all MEF Carrier Ethernet standards is to standardize services.

> **Carrier Ethernet** defines carrier services for a full spectrum of applications based on standardized technology-agnostic service definitions with Ethernet used as the standard interface for all services.

This full spectrum of carrier applications includes all applications, current and foreseen, that are supportable over Ethernet interfaces, including applications for IP access, wide area networking, and mobile backhaul. Carrier Ethernet even includes services to replace traditional Telecom services (circuit-based private line services).

Carrier Ethernet addresses all applications through services, not technology.

Carrier Ethernet services are defined in the abstract (independent of carrier network technology), so that carriers can implement services using any technologies they choose, except at the network edge.

---

3   In 2015, the MEF voted to change its official legal name from **Metro Ethernet Forum** to **MEF Forum**.

At the network edge, Carrier Ethernet requires IEEE 802.3 physical Ethernet technology to be used (in order to standardize the interface between the customer and the carrier), but Carrier Ethernet services are otherwise agnostic with respect to networking technology.

Why? What is the Motivation?

Carrier Ethernet is motivated by:

- The evolution of demands placed on carrier networking (from telephone services to data services)

- Commercial forces driving carriers toward a common cost-effective solution for data services

Since the 1980s, the demand for data services has grown, and the demand for circuit services has diminished. Prior to 1980, carrier networks (then called Telecom networks) used only circuit-based technology because telephone service (the only service of commercial interest at that time) is efficiently carried by circuits. But then computers and computer networking technology emerged, creating more and more demand for carrier networks to carry computer data between network locations.

Computer communication is fundamentally different from voice (telephone) communication because computers communicate through packets of information that are exchanged sporadically, rather than through continuous signals. Circuit-based technology can be adapted to support computer communication, but not very efficiently because circuits applied for data communication tend to be idle too much of the time.

Recognizing this inefficiency, a variety of technologies (such as X.25, Frame Relay, and ATM) were developed to support packet-based communication over carrier networks using computer networking principles, rather than dedicated circuits. Instead of using the network to create dedicated circuits (one for each communication session), these technologies allowed the network to be used more like a public road system. They allow packetized data from many services and customers to share the carrier network like cars share the highway. Services based on these technologies are less costly because they, in effect, provide access to a shared road system instead of exclusive use of a particular road within the system. Their wide-scale deployment in carrier networks has proven that packet-based technology can meet the requirements of carrier networking data service applications and is cost effective compared to circuit-based technology.

However, these cost-effective technology-specific services (X.25–, Frame Relay–, and ATM–based services) come with hidden costs to the customer (the enterprise that purchases the service). The customer has to place operationally complex devices (specialized routers) in their own networks and find resources in their own networking group to understand, provision, operate, and maintain them. Specialized expertise is not a problem in carrier networking, where technology is expected to be more specialized, but it can be a problem in customer networks, which are usually supported by more generic networking professionals.

Recognizing this issue, the prevailing philosophy is now to locate operationally complex components only in the carrier network (none in the customer network) and, additionally, to use IEEE 802.3 physical Ethernet as the standard interface between the carrier network and the customer network. Standardizing this interface allows carrier services to be defined abstractly, independent of whatever technology is used to implement the service in the carrier network.

Carrier Ethernet embraces this philosophy.

1.2.2
Elements of the Carrier Ethernet Services

Carrier Ethernet services are defined by a rich system of requirements (codified in MEF standards) developed by MEF experts and stakeholders to satisfy a range of objectives. At a high level, these objectives include:

- Defining services that are flexible enough to support the full spectrum of envisioned applications

- Defining services that are easy to understand and practical to use from the customer's perspective

- Defining services that carriers can provide using any kind of appropriate networking technology (except at the network edge, where Ethernet technology is required)

- Defining services that allow carriers to realize improved networking efficiency, compared to circuit-based technology, through the use of packet-based networking technologies

The particulars of any actual Carrier Ethernet service are specified in a service agreement (a contract) between the service subscriber (the customer) and the service provider (the carrier) that specifies service commitments in accordance with MEF standards. The service agreement, in effect, defines the limits of acceptable service behavior, not how it is implemented (or even, sometimes, its precise behavior).

Carrier Ethernet services include the following elements:

- **Connectivity** – Carrier Ethernet offers three service types (E-Line, E-LAN, and E-Tree) to support three forms of connectivity (point-to-point, multipoint-to-multipoint, and rooted-multipoint) between customer locations.

- **Service Multiplexing** – Carrier Ethernet supports port-based services (EPL, EP-LAN, and EP-Tree services) that cannot share service interfaces with other services, and VLAN-based services (EVPL, EVP-LAN, and EVP-Tree services) that can share service interfaces with other services. When an interface is shared by more than one service, it is said to support service multiplexing. Service multiplexing helps customers and carriers to save on customer network ports.

- **Quality of Service (QoS)** – Carrier Ethernet services include a rich system of QoS options. Service performance is specified in the service agreement using performance objectives (agreed values for MEF-defined performance metrics which, in turn, are used to evaluate things like service availability, reliability, frame loss, and frame delay). A Carrier Ethernet service can include more than one QoS traffic stream.

- **Bandwidth Profiles** – The amount of traffic that a Carrier Ethernet service supports is specified in the service agreement using bandwidth profiles. A bandwidth profile is a set of values that govern operation of an algorithm for measuring traffic flow at a given point. The bandwidth profile, in effect, sets limits on how much traffic the service will support, but it sets these limits in a relatively sophisticated way. Roughly, it includes two limits: one limit for continuous traffic and another limit that allows traffic to "burst" beyond the continuous traffic limit. Excess traffic beyond both limits (the continuous limit and the burst limit) is declared to be **red** and is dropped. Traffic that is not dropped can be admitted to the service in two categories: **green** (committed traffic, subject to performance objectives) and **yellow** (excess traffic, not subject to performance objectives).

- **Operations, Administration and Management (OAM)** – Carrier Ethernet OAM support includes mechanisms for fault detection, troubleshooting, and performance monitoring of individual services.

1.2.3
Example Carrier Ethernet Service Applications

Let's look at three representative examples that roughly illustrate the range of possible Carrier Ethernet service applications:

1. IP Access application

2. Virtual Private Network (VPN) application

3. Circuit Emulation Service over Ethernet (CESoETH) application

IP Access Application

The customer wants to connect their local network to an **internet service provider (ISP)** to gain Web access, e-mail, and similar IP services. To accomplish this, the customer, in concert with the ISP, purchases a point-to-point Carrier Ethernet service and uses that service to connect an Ethernet switch (or IP router) in the customer network to a router in the ISP network (both have Ethernet interfaces).

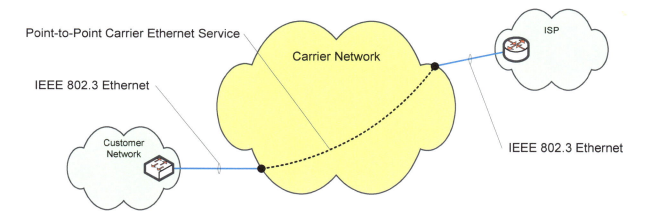

The point-to-point service provides connectivity through the carrier network that is functionally similar to connecting Ethernet ports with a very long Ethernet cable. However, connectivity is not really through dedicated hardware. It is through a service implemented over the carrier network, and carriers will generally implement this service using packet-based technology (for efficiency), which means the service will share and compete for resources within the network with other services.

Primary concerns for all Carrier Ethernet services are to define how much traffic the service will support (service bandwidth) and qualities of the service, such as speed of delivery and reliability of delivery.

In IP access applications, quality of service (QoS) requirements can be very modest. Often, "best-effort" QoS is acceptable, which means the carrier agrees to try to deliver all traffic (up to agreed bandwidth limits), but is allowed to drop traffic if there is network congestion. Best-effort QoS can be acceptable to customers because it is less costly and because many computer networking applications (such as Internet and e-mail) are fault tolerant and not time sensitive.

Virtual Private Network Application

The customer has local networks at three or more locations (three in this example) and wants to interconnect them through the carrier network to establish a single aggregate network. The resulting network, called a **virtual private network (VPN)**, can be established in several ways.

Partial-Mesh Solution

One approach is to purchase point-to-point Carrier Ethernet services to connect Ethernet switch ports (and/or IP router ports) through the carrier network. The following example shows hub-and-spoke connectivity established using two point-to-point Carrier Ethernet services.

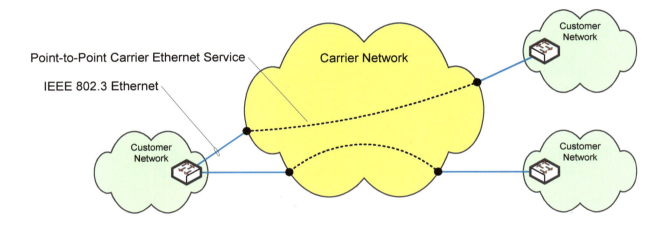

Full-Mesh Solution

Alternatively, full-mesh connectivity can be established using three point-to-point Carrier Ethernet services.

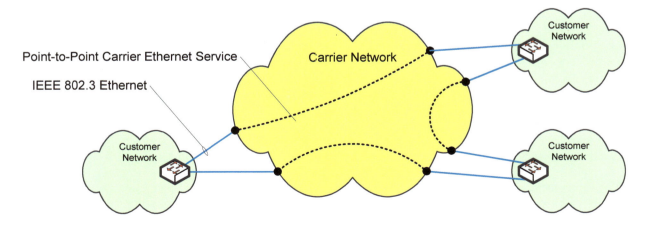

In either case, each point-to-point service provides connectivity through the carrier network that is functionally similar to connecting Ethernet ports with a very long Ethernet cable.

Multipoint-to-Multipoint Solution

Another approach is to use a single multipoint-to-multipoint Carrier Ethernet service.

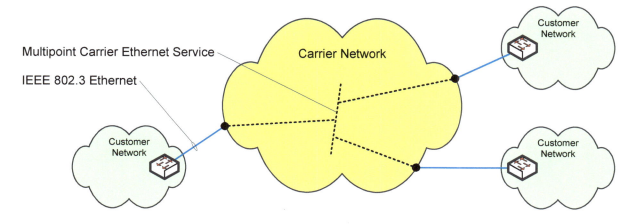

A multipoint-to-multipoint Carrier Ethernet service provides connectivity that is functionally similar to connecting the networks to an Ethernet switch (or LAN segment) within the carrier network.

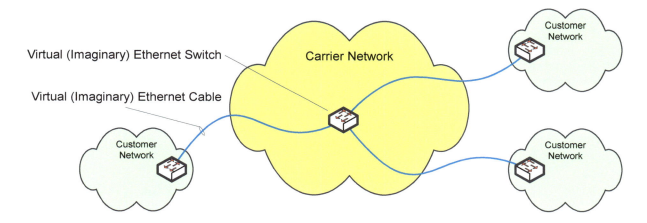

At a high level all of these solutions are easily understood by the customer's networking professionals because they mimic familiar modes of network connection (using Ethernet cables and/or Ethernet switches). However, connectivity is not really through dedicated hardware. It is through services implemented over the carrier network, and carriers will generally implement these services using packet-based technology (for efficiency), which means these services share resources within the network with other services.

Primary concerns for both the customer and the carrier are to define how much traffic the service will support (service bandwidth) and qualities of the service, such as speed of delivery and reliability of delivery.

CESoETH Application

In this application, the customer wants to replace a traditional circuit-based Telecom service (a T1 line service in this example) with an equivalent Carrier Ethernet service. To accomplish this, the customer purchases a point-to-point Carrier Ethernet service and connects that service to special generic interworking function (GIWF) equipment in their networks that, in turn, connects to PBX (Private Branch Exchange) equipment as shown in the following figure.

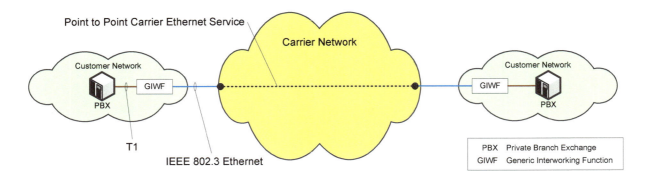

This type of service, called Circuit Emulation Service over Ethernet (CESoETH), requires specialized equipment (a pair of GIWF devices) to be used in combination with the point-to-point Carrier Ethernet service. These devices can be located in the customer network, as shown, or in the carrier network.

The MEF defines CESoETH service standards separately from Carrier Ethernet service standards. CESoETH service standards do not change Carrier Ethernet service standards in any way. They adapt them, through augmentation with GIWF, to support circuit services.

The point-to-point Carrier Ethernet service required for this application is defined like any other point-to-point Carrier Ethernet service, except that it is tailored to meet very high QoS requirements, consistent with circuit-based TDM technology, so that the resulting CESoETH service is indistinguishable from a T1 line service from the PBX perspective.

This example highlights an application of Carrier Ethernet that is very time-sensitive and fault intolerant.

If the carrier network uses packet-based technology (for efficiency), this kind of service must be given priority over other services, which share and compete with this service for network resources.

2
Ethernet in Local Area Networking

In this chapter:

A **local area network (LAN)** is a computer network that spans a relatively small area. Most LANs are confined to a single building or group of buildings; however, one LAN can be connected to other LANs over any distance by various means (telephone lines, radio waves, Carrier Ethernet service). A system of LANs connected in this way is called a wide area network (WAN).

Thanks to vigorous commercial development, Ethernet LANs are now implemented using a variety of technologies and devices, allowing hundreds or even thousands of computers to communicate through a single LAN.

Goals of this chapter include:

- To provide a basic understanding of how an Ethernet LAN operates

- To illustrate different methods of implementing an Ethernet LAN

- To explain the limitations and evolution of Ethernet LAN technologies

- To introduce the concept of a virtual LAN (VLAN), which is logical LAN connectivity that emulates physical LAN connectivity

---

Ethernet LAN technology, described in this chapter, lays a foundation for understanding Ethernet in all contexts, including in the Carrier Ethernet context. This technology is familiar to all enterprise[4] networking professionals. Carrier Ethernet professionals need to understand it to clearly understand Carrier Ethernet applications from the customer perspective.

---

4   **Enterprise**— Any organization, such as a business, a non-profit, a university, or a government agency.

2.1
Ethernet Fundamentals

In this section:

Computer networks are designed to support communication between any two computers that are connected through the network and to make it easy to add or remove computers. Ideally computers are added to a network in plug-and-play fashion or something very close to that ideal. General computer networking is beyond the scope of this book, but a rough model is required to understand how Ethernet fits into the big picture.

What is a computer? — In the context of computer networking, a computer is any device that communicates through the network with other similar devices (computers), for example, a PC, a server, or a printer.

What is communication? — Communication is the exchange of information (data) between processes running on different computers. Examples include making a request, acknowledging a request, replying to a request, transferring data for printing or processing.

2.1.1
OSI Reference Model

The field of computer networking has universally embraced the use of layered reference models to describe computer networking architectures. There are many layered models, but the 7-layer Open Systems Interconnect (OSI) reference model is the de facto high-level reference model against which communication protocols[5] are commonly classified.[6]

In the OSI reference model, communication between computers involves up to 7 layers of processes running on each computer. Only the first three layers of the OSI reference model are of much interest to Carrier Ethernet:

- **Layer 1** deals with the transmission of a bit stream over physical media (such as over electrical cable or fiber-optic cable or through radio waves). Layer 1 is essential for any communication. Traditional TDM-based Telecom technology includes only Layer 1 technology.

- **Layer 2** is of most interest because Carrier Ethernet services are defined at Layer 2.

- **Layer 3** is important because Ethernet networks terminate at devices operating at Layer 3 or higher.

OSI Model

Data Unit	Layer	
	Data	7. Application
Host Layers	Data	6. Presentation
	Data	5. Session
	Segments	4. Transport
Media Layers	Packets	3. Network
	Frames	2. Data Link
	Bits	1. Physical

---

5 **Communications protocol** — A system of digital message formats and rules for exchanging messages in or between computing systems
6 Networking communication typically involves less than 7 OSI layers. Only the lowest 3 or 4 layers get much attention. The OSI reference model is generally understood to provide a rough (but well-known) framework for talking about layered networking, rather than a rigidly defined standard.

Within each computer that is in communication, each layer interacts only with adjacent layers (the process above it and/or the process below it). Data is passed using standard formats called **protocol data units (PDUs)**.

PDU Encapsulation and De-encapsulation

At Layer 2, the PDU includes a header, a trailer, and data between the header and the trailer. At all other layers the PDU includes a header followed by data. The data within each PDU (excluding the top layer PDU) <u>is</u> the next higher-layer PDU.

Outgoing data moves downward through the layers. Incoming data moves upward. In transition between layers, one of two processes occurs:

- **Encapsulation** — A header (or a header and a trailer) is added to the outgoing data to create a new lower-layer PDU.

- **De-encapsulation** — A header (or a header and a trailer) is removed from an incoming PDU to extract data (the next higher-layer PDU).

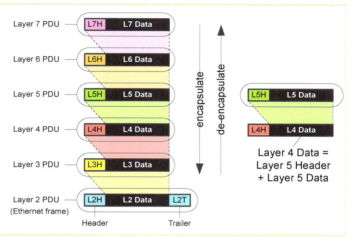

Adjacent Layer Interaction

On each computer:

Each process (excluding the top-layer process) provides a service to the process directly above it.

Each process (excluding the Layer 1 process) uses the process directly below it like a mail utility (or mailbox):

- It hands data off to the next lower-layer process for transfer to another computer.

- It receives data (sent from other computers) through the next lower-layer process.

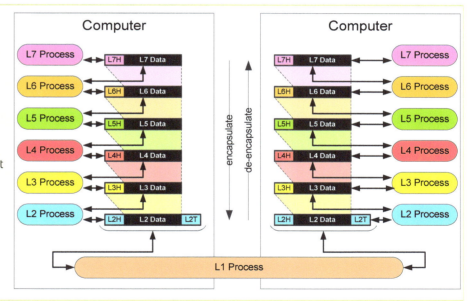

This layered architecture simplifies development by relieving each layer from details that are handled by lower layers. The Layer 1 process physically transfers the Layer 2 PDUs (within a bit stream) between computers.

Same Layer Interaction

Layered architecture also allows developers and operators to focus on one layer at a time. From this perspective, Layer-n processes on different computers are peers that communicate directly with each other using the Layer-n PDU.

At each layer, lower layer processes are assumed to operate correctly. The resulting abstract view of reality greatly simplifies development and troubleshooting.

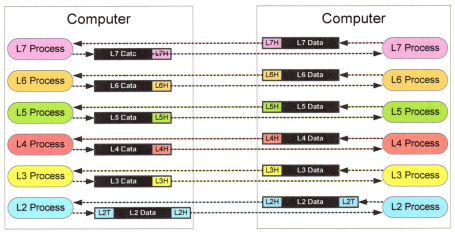

Classification of Network Devices

The 7-Layer OSI reference model is commonly used to classify network devices (defined later in this book).

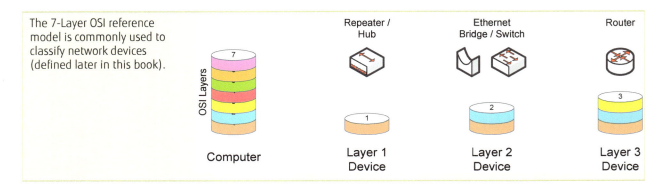

A computer is a device on the edge of the network (such as a PC, a printer, or a server) that the computer network is designed to support.

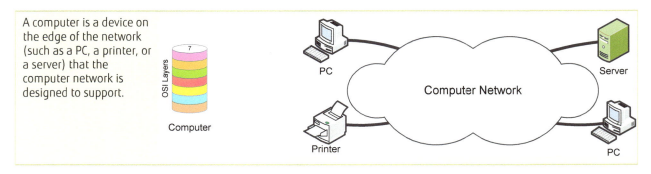

Computers[7] potentially operate using all seven OSI layers. Devices inside the network are classified according to their highest OSI layer of operation: Layer 1, 2, or 3.

---

7 The OSI reference model uses the term **end station**, instead of **computer**. This book uses the term computer to avoid confusion with Ethernet end stations.

A Layer 1 device, such as a repeater or an Ethernet hub (defined later in this book), passes a digital signal from one port or channel to another (or possibly to more than one different ports or channels).

Note: Here, the term **digital signal** *refers to a series of bits or a bit stream. The bit stream includes data (which the device does not modify) and other bits, called* **overhead***, used for Layer 1 processing (which the device may modify).*

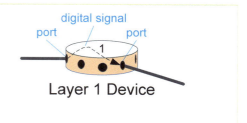

A Layer 1 device might do many sophisticated things with a signal (multiplexing/demultiplexing, broadcasting, translation from one transmission medium to another, and so on), but a Layer 1 device does not look for, or see, Layer 2 PDUs within the signal.

A Layer 2 device, such as an Ethernet bridge or switch (defined later in this book), identifies Layer 2 PDUs (Ethernet frames) and forwards them individually based on protocol. Bridging (a core topic in this book) is a Layer 2 process.

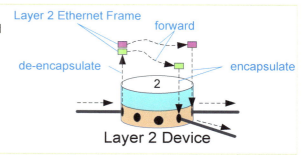

Layer 3 devices, known as routers, forward Layer 3 PDUs (packets) based on routing protocols (which are not explained in this book[8]).

From the Layer-2 perspective, routers are significant because they (like any device operating above layer 2) are edge devices with respect to Layer 2 networking.

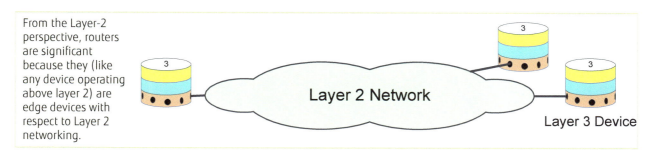

Note: *This OSI-based system of device classification is based on functionality that is actually used. Real commercial devices can sometimes support multiple applications simultaneously. For example, a physical device might act as a Layer 2 device for one application while acting as a Layer 3 device for other applications.*

Related Links

Ethernet Hub LAN on p. 28
MAC Bridging / Layer 2 Switching on p. 30
Ethernet with IP Routing on p. 105

---

8 The appendix includes an explanation of Ethernet in IP routing, but IP routing itself is beyond the scope of this book.

Defining the Layer 2 Network

If a router (a Layer 3 device) is interior to a network, the network is not a Layer 2 network. In this example, four computers (two PCs, a printer, and a server) are connected through a general computer network of hubs (Layer 1), bridges/switches (Layer 2), and routers (Layer 3).

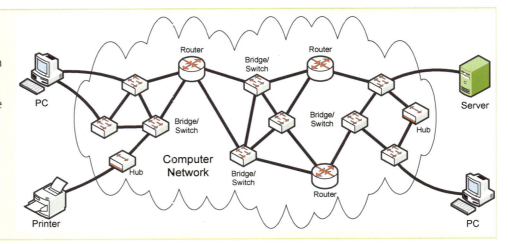

From the OSI model perspective, the network looks like this.

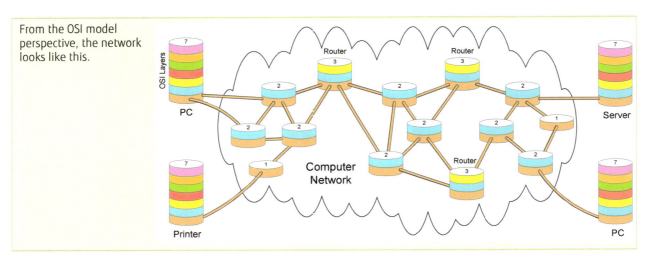

From a Layer 2 perspective, this network is composed of three Layer 2 networks.

If Ethernet is used, each Layer 2 network is also an Ethernet network.

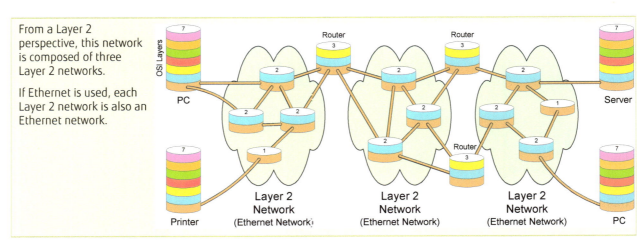

2.1.2
Ethernet

Ethernet technology is defined over two layers (Layer 1 and Layer 2) in the OSI reference model. Sometimes, however, the Layer 1 component of Ethernet is taken for granted as part of Layer 1 processing.

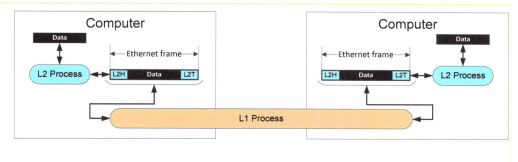

Generally, the term Ethernet (without qualification) refers to Layer 2 Ethernet as standalone networking technology.

Ethernet End Station

An Ethernet end station is an <u>interface</u> on the edge of an Ethernet network.

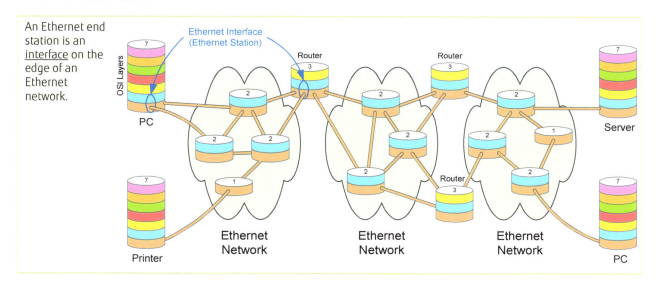

Notice that routers and computers can have more than one interface to an Ethernet network. Each interface is an Ethernet end station.

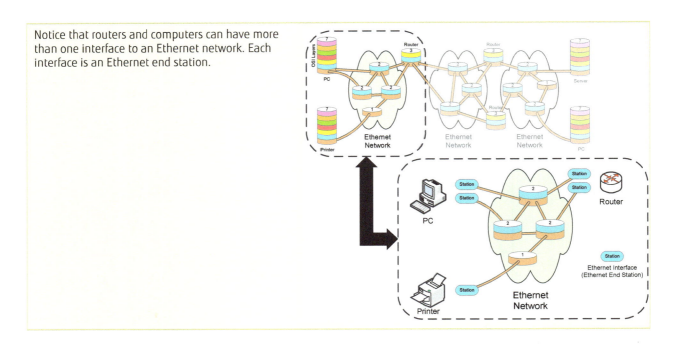

2.1.3
Ethernet Communication

The main purpose of an Ethernet network is to transfer **Ethernet frames**[9] between Ethernet end stations that interconnect through the network.

At a high level, an Ethernet network works somewhat like the postal service: an Ethernet frame is addressed to a destination, and the network delivers the frame to the destination.

Each end device connects to the network through one or more interfaces called **Ethernet end stations**. Each Ethernet end station (interface) has a globally unique identifier known as its **MAC address** (Media Access Control address). No two Ethernet interfaces in the world have the same MAC address.

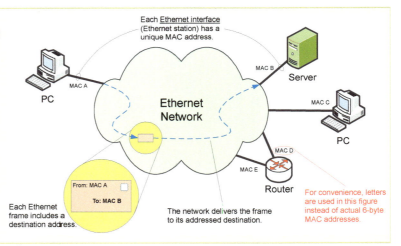

Note: *Other names sometimes used in place of **MAC address** include Ethernet address, NIC (network interface card) address, and LAN address.*

---

9 Some people use the term **Ethernet packet** in place of **Ethernet frame**. The term **Ethernet frame** is preferred because it complies with terminology defined in the Transmission Control Protocol/Internet Protocol (TCP/IP) networking reference model. TCP/IP is another layered computer networking model, like the OSI model, but more specialized. According to the TCP/IP reference model, Layer 2 protocol data unit (PDUs) are called frames, and Layer 3 PDUs are called packets.

Every Ethernet frame includes a destination MAC address that generally[10] specifies an individual Ethernet end station to which the frame is to be delivered. The network's job is to deliver Ethernet frames. This postal model for frame delivery is pretty good, but it is only a starting point. Ethernet differs as follows:

- Not all destination MAC addresses correspond to unique Ethernet end stations. Those that do are called **unicast** MAC addresses. Other types of destination MAC addresses, known as **broadcast** and **multicast** MAC addresses, will be explained later.

- The network might actually deliver the Ethernet frame to other (untargeted) Ethernet end stations (not just to the addressed unicast destination).[11]

The real model for unicast frame delivery <u>allows</u> frames to go to other Ethernet end stations (not just to the addressed unicast destination). However, the end result is the same because each Ethernet end station is <u>required to discard</u> all unicast frames that are not addressed to itself.

Unicast Ethernet frames do not <u>necessarily</u> go to extra destinations, but they can. Actual delivery depends on how the network is implemented and on the network state (as will be explained later).

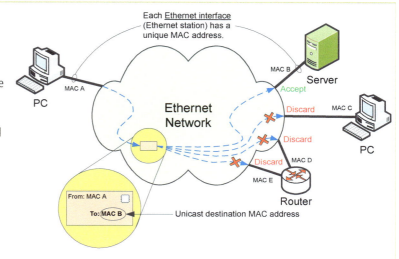

Key points:

- An Ethernet end station is an interface (not a device).

- Each Ethernet end station has a unique MAC address.

- To communicate, an Ethernet end station simply transmits a properly addressed Ethernet frame into the network.

- Each Ethernet end station may receive unicast frames that are not addressed to itself. If this happens, the Ethernet end station must discard them.

So far nothing has been said about how an Ethernet network operates because there are various implementations (explained later in this book) that operate differently. However, all implementations support communication between Ethernet end stations without establishing circuits or connections between Ethernet end stations (Ethernet is a connectionless protocol). All implementations also make it easy to add or remove Ethernet end stations (ideally in plug-and-play fashion, or something very close to that ideal).

Related Links

Ethernet End Station on p. 21
MAC Addresses on p. 25

---

10 Some destination MAC addresses (broadcast and multicast addresses) are reserved for special purposes that will be explained later.
  11 Unlike a postal letter or package, an Ethernet frame is easily copied (replicated), which allows multiple Ethernet end stations to receive the same Ethernet frame.

2.1.4
Ethernet Frame

At Layer 2, an Ethernet frame includes a header, a trailer, and data between the header and the trailer. The header is sent first, followed by the data (typically a Layer 3 PDU), followed by the trailer.

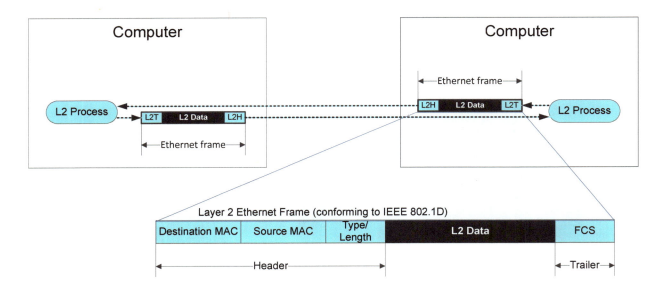

The header includes three fields, sent in the following order:

- **Destination MAC Address** — A 6-byte field containing the address of the target destination(s) of the frame

- **Source MAC Address** — A 6-byte field containing the address of the Ethernet end station that sent the frame

- **Type/Length** — A 2-byte field that defines either the length of the data field or the type of protocol listed inside the frame

The trailer consists of one 4-byte field called the **frame check sequence (FCS)**, which is used for error detection.

Note: *At this stage, we consider only IEEE 802.1D–compliant Ethernet frames, the baseline Ethernet frame format that is used in LANs and for MAC Bridging. Frame formats for VLAN Bridging and Provider Bridging include additional fields for VLAN tagging.*

Related Links

OSI Reference Model on p. 16
Ethernet on p. 21
MAC Addresses on p. 25

MAC Addresses

Media access control addresses (MAC addresses) come from a 48-bit address space containing nearly 300 trillion MAC addresses. For human recognition, a MAC address is represented by 6 groups of 2 hexadecimal digits:

MAC address = XX:XX:XX:XX:XX:XX

Where each X represents a hexadecimal digit from the set {0, 1, 2, 3, 4, 5, 6, 7, 8, 9, A, B, C, D, E, F}

Example: *00:0A:95:9D:68:16*

Every Ethernet frame contains two MAC addresses: a **destination MAC address** (the target) and a **source MAC address** (the sender).

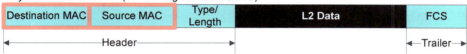

The **destination MAC address** does not always target an individual Ethernet interface. If it does, it is called a **unicast** MAC address. Otherwise, it is a **multicast** or **broadcast** MAC address.

Unicast address – Targets a single Ethernet end station

If the second hexadecimal digit is even (0, 2, 4, 6, 8, A, C, or E), the address is a unicast MAC address.

Example: *00:0A:95:9D:68:16*

Multicast address – Targets a group of interfaces that are provisioned to accept the address

If the second hexadecimal digit is odd (1, 3, 5, 7, 9, B, D, or F), the address is a multicast or broadcast MAC address.

Example: *01:0A:95:9D:68:16*

Broadcast address – Targets all Ethernet interfaces in the network

Example: *FF:FF:FF:FF:FF:FF*

The **source MAC address** always corresponds to a unique sender (the Ethernet end station that originated the frame) and consequently conforms to the unicast address space.

For a given Ethernet end station, the following three MAC addresses match: (1) the factory assigned MAC address of the Ethernet end station, (2) the source MAC address of any Ethernet frame sent from the Ethernet end station, and (3) the destination MAC address of any unicast Ethernet frame sent to the Ethernet end station.

The appendix explains MAC addressing in more detail.

Related Links

MAC Addressing in Detail on p. 94
Spanning Tree Protocols on p. 40

Layer 1 Processing of Ethernet Frames

Note: *IEEE 802.3 defines Layer 1 Ethernet technology that supports IEEE 802.1 (Layer 2 Ethernet Technology).*

The Layer 1 Ethernet process mediates between the Layer 2 Ethernet process and the network:

- **Transmit** — Ethernet frames received from the Layer 2 process are encoded in the outgoing bit stream and transmitted to the network.

- **Receive** — Ethernet frames are extracted from the incoming bit stream and passed to the Layer 2 process.

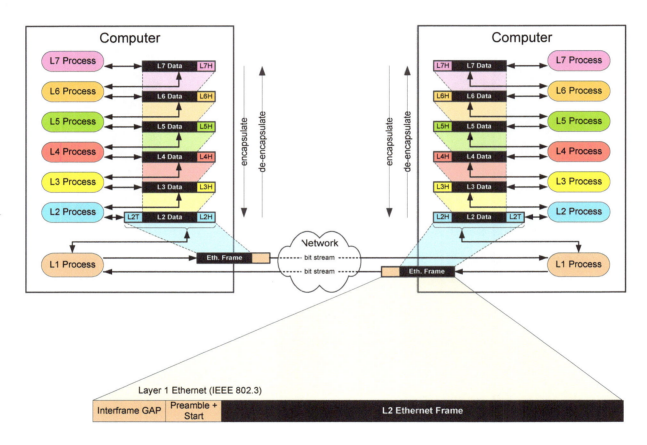

In the Layer 1 bit stream, each Layer 2 Ethernet frame is preceded by two fields sent in the following order:

1. **Interframe GAP** — At least 12 bytes of silence (a sequence of at least 96 bits that are either all 1s or all 0s)

2. **Preamble + Start** — An 8-byte field containing a *Preamble* (7 bytes, each containing the bit pattern 10101010) followed by a *Start of Frame Delimiter* (1 byte containing byte sequence 10101011, which denotes the start of the frame itself)

2.2
Shared Media Ethernet

In this section:

Ethernet LANs were originally implemented using shared media: first with coaxial cable, then using a device called the Ethernet hub. Both forms require Ethernet end stations to run a protocol, called CSMA/CD (Carrier Sense Multiple Access with Collision Detection), to coordinate sharing.

2.2.1
Coaxial Cable LAN

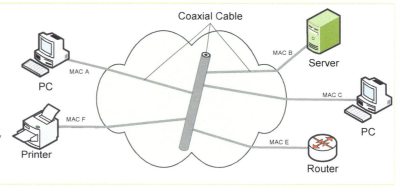

Ethernet LANs were first implemented using coaxial cable. A length of coaxial cable was routed through the building and Ethernet end stations were connected into it using coaxial cable. The resulting connection constitutes an electrical bus (supporting one voltage) that is shared by the Ethernet end stations.

Note: *Coaxial cable LANs are no longer used, but still serve as an important conceptual touchstone.*

Each Ethernet end station can control the voltage on the bus (transmit bits) and read the voltage from the bus (receive bits), but cannot transmit and receive at the same time (communication is **half duplex**[12]).

Functionally, the result is like a telephone teleconference. Each party (Ethernet end station) can talk (transmit) and listen (receive) at any time. However, for effective communication, only one party (Ethernet end station) should talk (transmit) at a time because everything said (transmitted) is broadcast for all parties to hear (receive). If two end stations transmit at the same time, the signal received by all end stations is corrupted. A special protocol, called CSMA/CD (described later in this book), runs on each Ethernet end station to overcome the problem of multiple Ethernet end stations trying to transmit at the same time.

---

12   A system that supports communication in both directions but in only one direction at a time (not simultaneously) is **half duplex**.

Unicast frame delivery is supported as follows. One Ethernet end station transmits the Ethernet frame into the network. The network, in effect, broadcasts the Ethernet frame to all other stations. If an Ethernet end station receives a frame that is addressed to itself, it accepts the frame. Otherwise, it discards the frame.

Coaxial cable LAN implementation is now rare, but the fishbone graphic that derives from it is commonly used to represent a LAN, or LAN segment, symbolically.

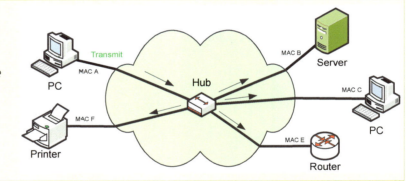

Note: *Representation of a LAN, or LAN segment, with a fishbone graphic does not imply coaxial cable implementation; it simply indicates LAN functionality.*

2.2.2
Ethernet Hub LAN

An Ethernet hub is a multiport device that functions like the coaxial cable LAN but is easier to deploy and provides better signal quality over greater distances.

Note: *Ethernet end stations connect to the hub through an appropriate standardized Ethernet cable, typically an unshielded twisted pair (UTP) cable with RJ-45 connectors.*

Like the coaxial cable LAN, the hub LAN:

- Receives a signal from any Ethernet end station and broadcasts it to all other end stations

- Provides one transmission channel that is shared by all Ethernet end stations

- Requires each Ethernet end station to run CSMA/CD (described later in this book) to overcome the problem of multiple Ethernet end stations trying to transmit at the same time

Unicast frame delivery is supported in the same way that it is supported in the coaxial cable LAN. One Ethernet end station transmits the Ethernet frame into the network. The network broadcasts the Ethernet frame to all other stations. If the Ethernet frame is addressed to the receiving station, the frame is accepted. Otherwise, the frame is discarded.

The Ethernet hub has no Layer 2 functionality. It does not buffer Ethernet frames or look at MAC addresses. It is a Layer 1 device that typically transmits bits through a single shared electrical bus (internal to the hub).

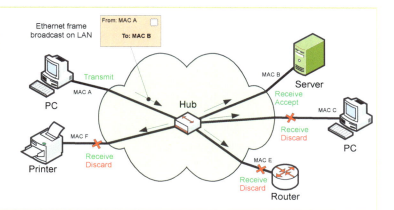

2.2.3
CSMA/CD and Transmission Collisions

Carrier Sense Multiple Access with Collision Detection (CSMA/CD)[13] is the protocol that Ethernet end stations use to communicate when they are connected through shared media (by coaxial cable LAN or Ethernet hub LAN). Because there is only one channel for communication, only one Ethernet end station can transmit at a time. Otherwise, the signal received by all end stations is corrupted.

CSMA/CD works roughly like this:
1. When a station has an Ethernet frame ready to transmit, it checks to see if the shared channel is already in use. If the channel is in use, the station waits until the channel is free. Otherwise, the station begins transmission.
2. While transmitting, the station "listens" to the signal received on the shared channel to ensure that it matches its own transmission. If the signals match, there is no problem (no other station is transmitting at the same time), and the station continues transmitting the Ethernet frame. Otherwise, there is a **transmission collision** (another station is also transmitting). If this happens, the station stops transmitting and waits a "random" back off period of time before trying again to resend the same Ethernet frame, using the same process starting from scratch.

The "random" back off period is key to avoiding repeated collisions. Because each station involved in the collision waits a different amount of time (the "random" back off period) before trying to transmit again, the chance of re-collision is low.

2.2.4
Summary

Shared media Ethernet works very well for small computer networks. It allows small networks to be easily built and new computers to be added in plug-and-play fashion. However, practical issues limit network size:

- **Limited bandwidth** – CSMA/CD enables end stations to share the media, but the shared media has limited bandwidth and all end stations inevitably share that bandwidth.

- **Collisions** – Networking efficiency decreases as network size increases because collisions occur more frequently as more and more end stations compete for the single shared transmission channel.

- **Malfunctioning end stations** – A single malfunctioning end station can bring down the entire network by sending continuous transmissions to the shared media, hogging the shared media bandwidth.

Shared media LANs cannot guarantee that any amount of bandwidth is available to any individual end station.

---

13 Refer to IEEE 802.3 2008 Part 3: Carrier Sense Multiple Access with Collision Detection (CSMA/CD).

2.3
MAC Bridging / Layer 2 Switching

In this section:

As shared media Ethernet became popular, LANs grew in number. Individual LANs grew in size, but only up to a point because collision issues forced large LANs to be broken up into smaller LANs. Many small LANs existed in isolation from each other, and this created a demand for some way to connect them.

MAC bridging was developed to increase effective LAN size over what can be achieved using shared media technology (coaxial cable LAN technology or hub LAN technology) alone. MAC bridging allows two or more shared media LANs to be interconnected, through a **bridge**, to create a larger LAN that is less vulnerable to transmission collisions (previously described). Collisions occur <u>within</u> each shared media LAN as previously described, but not <u>between</u> end stations that are in different shared media LANs.

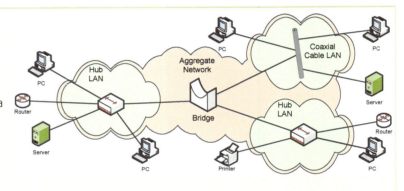

MAC bridges were first implemented in software (running on generic computer hardware), then later using specialized commercial hardware (Ethernet switches).

A MAC bridge can connect both LANs and individual Ethernet end stations.

This should not be surprising, considering that an individual end station might connect through a LAN that includes no other end stations.

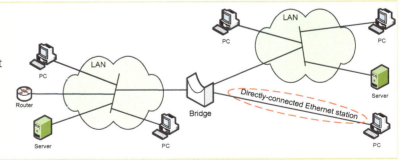

Related Links

Shared Media Ethernet on p. 27
LANs and LAN Segments (Collision Domains) on p. 35

2.3.1
MAC Bridging

MAC bridging, defined by the IEEE 802.1D standard, involves two components: **MAC address learning** and **frame forwarding**. Before explaining these components, let's explain their effect in a simple example.

Example Application

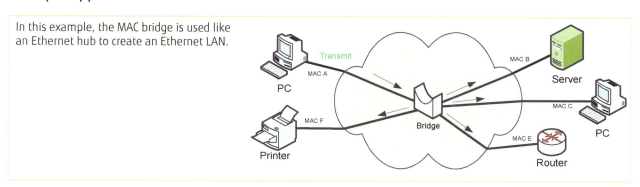

In this example, the MAC bridge is used like an Ethernet hub to create an Ethernet LAN.

The MAC bridge is similar to the Ethernet hub in several ways:

- It can receive an Ethernet frame on any port.

- It can transmit received Ethernet frames out other ports.

- Devices connect to the MAC bridge through a standardized Ethernet cable, typically a UTP cable with RJ-45 connectors.

However, the MAC bridge provides additional functionality:

- It supports **full duplex**[14] communication, allowing each Ethernet end station to transmit and receive simultaneously.

- It can recognize and process Ethernet frames (because it is a Layer 2 device).

- It can buffer Ethernet frames (temporarily store them in memory).

- It can forward Ethernet frames intelligently based on MAC address learning.

Every port of a MAC bridge is an Ethernet interface and has a unique factory-assigned MAC address. However, unlike an Ethernet end station (which only accepts frames addressed to itself), each MAC bridge port runs in **promiscuous** mode, which allows it to receive all Ethernet frames, regardless of MAC address.

Because the MAC bridge can buffer Ethernet frames (store Ethernet frames temporarily in memory), the Ethernet end stations can transmit at the same time and do not have to run CSMA/CD.

---

14 A system that supports communication in both directions simultaneously is called **full duplex**.

MAC address learning (described later in this book) allows the bridge to learn which Ethernet end station is connected to each port. After learning, the bridge forwards Ethernet frames appropriately (only to the particular Ethernet end station to which the frame is addressed, rather than to all Ethernet end stations).

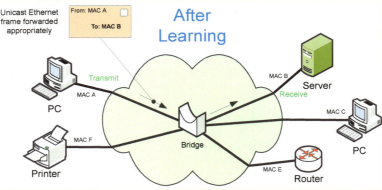

Before learning, however, the bridge broadcasts Ethernet frames to all Ethernet end stations (in effect, similar to the hub LAN or coaxial cable LAN). Thus, each Ethernet end station may still receive Ethernet frames that are not addressed to itself, that it then must discard.

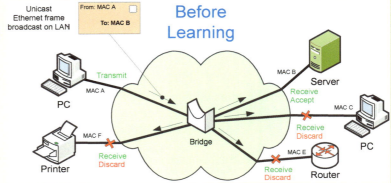

Note: *Application of the bridge to implement a LAN is perfectly valid. However, the bridge was originally invented to interconnect LANs such that the aggregation of LANs function like a single LAN.*

MAC Address Learning

Regardless of application, the bridge uses information gleaned from received frames to learn how to forward unicast frames in the future. Learned information is stored in a table called the **forwarding database** (or MAC address table). The forwarding database is the bridge's record of which Ethernet end stations can be reached on which ports.

Whenever a bridge receives an Ethernet frame, it notes two pieces of information:

*   The port on which the frame was received

*   The <u>source</u> MAC address in the Ethernet frame

If this information is not already in the forwarding database, it is stored there for future use.

Through this process of **MAC address learning**, the bridge gradually builds a forwarding database that lists the addresses of many Ethernet end stations and associates one port with each address.

The forwarding database in this example includes every Ethernet end station shown in the figure, except the one with MAC address B. This implies that the bridge has received at least one Ethernet frame from each Ethernet end station, except the one with MAC address B.

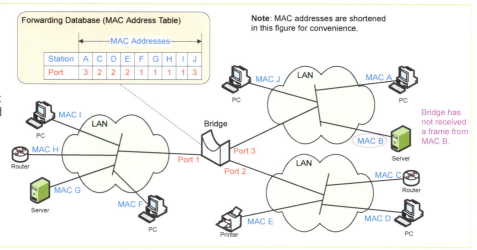

Related Links

MAC Addresses on p. 25
MAC Addressing in Detail on p. 94

Frame Forwarding

A bridge uses its forwarding database to intelligently forward Ethernet frames.

If the bridge receives a unicast frame with a destination address that **is not in the forwarding database**, it forwards the frame out all switch ports other than the one it was received on.

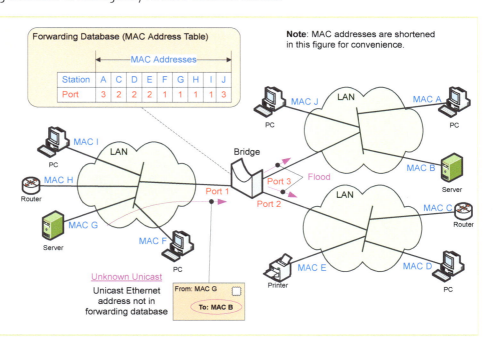

Such frames are called **unknown unicast frames**. The process of forwarding them out all other ports, called **flooding**[15], ensures that the frame is forwarded onward toward the target destination (assuming that destination is reachable).

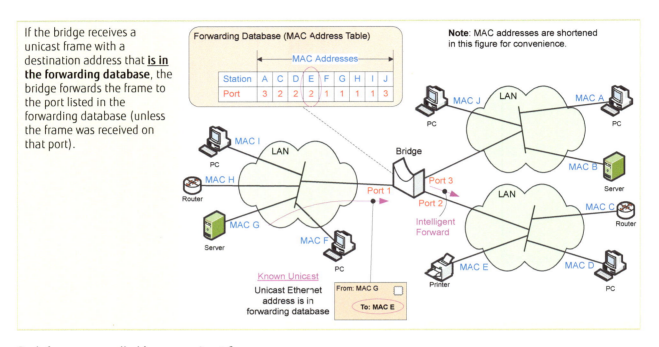

If the bridge receives a unicast frame with a destination address that **is in the forwarding database**, the bridge forwards the frame to the port listed in the forwarding database (unless the frame was received on that port).

Such frames are called **known unicast frames**.

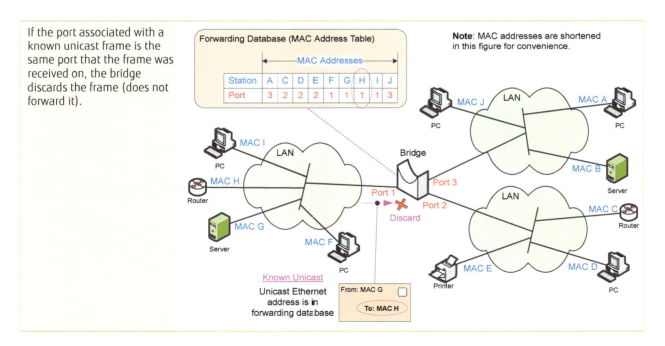

If the port associated with a known unicast frame is the same port that the frame was received on, the bridge discards the frame (does not forward it).

---

15   Flooding is equivalent to broadcasting.

LANs and LAN Segments (Collision Domains)

With MAC bridging, the aggregate network (the connected shared media LANs, plus the bridge) provides LAN connectivity for the complete set of Ethernet end stations (any station can communicate with any other station).

So, from the end station perspective, the aggregate network is simply another LAN.

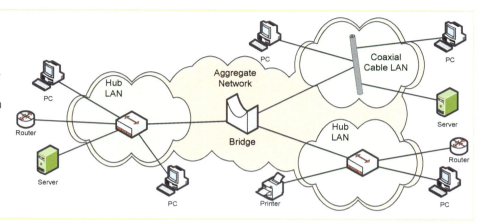

With bridging, the overall aggregate network becomes the LAN.

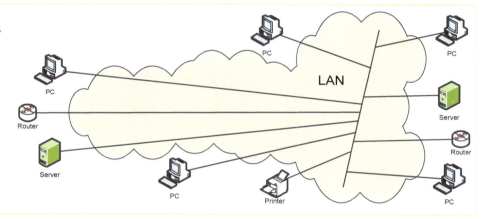

The subnetworks that are connected through the bridge are called **LAN segments** (or **collision domains** because transmission collisions within the LAN are confined to LAN segments).

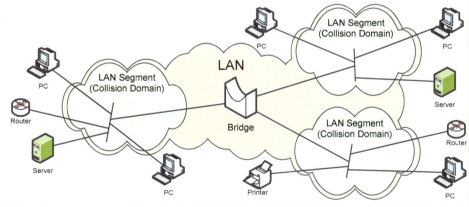

The bridge dramatically reduces traffic in the aggregate LAN through segmentation. The bridge filters traffic such that local unicast traffic (traffic between Ethernet end stations in the same LAN segment) is kept local, and non-local unicast traffic is forwarded intelligently (to the correct LAN segment, the one containing the target, and nowhere else).

Bridged LANs can themselves be aggregated, by connecting bridges, as shown in this example.

The resulting aggregated network is a LAN (any station can communicate with any other station) with two levels of LAN segmentation.

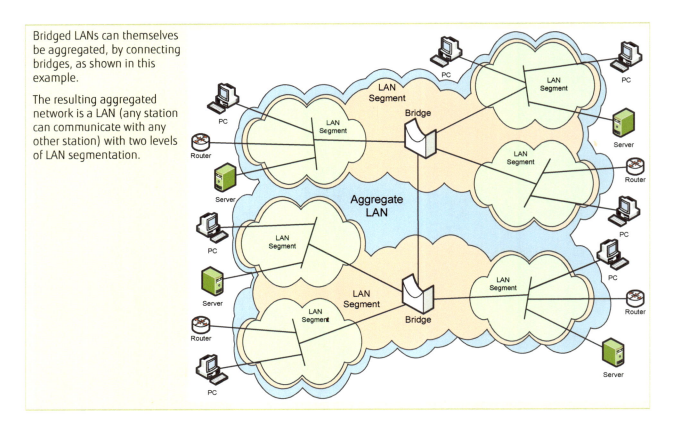

2.3.2
From Bridge to Switch

Bridging allowed LANs to grow bigger (compared to shared media LANs) and became very popular.

Commercial equipment suppliers developed specialized hardware, called Ethernet switches, to support it. Specialized bridging devices are marketed as Ethernet switches (rather than bridges) to emphasize high-performance frame forwarding (realized through dedicated hardware, rather than software).

The Ethernet switch evolved from an expensive device with only a few ports (for connecting only a few LAN segments) into a cheap device with many ports:

- Enough ports to provide each end station its own dedicated port (LAN segment)

- Cheap enough to use in place of the hub[16]

2.3.3
Bridge / Switch Interconnection

Bridge/switch interconnection can lead to serious traffic problems if the network topology includes any loops.

Loop-Free Networks

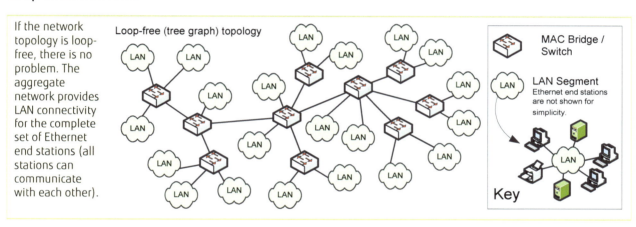

If the network topology is loop-free, there is no problem. The aggregate network provides LAN connectivity for the complete set of Ethernet end stations (all stations can communicate with each other).

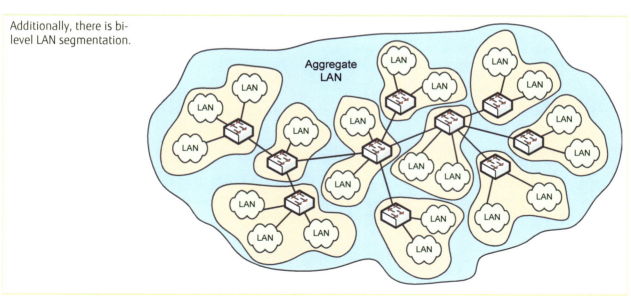

Additionally, there is bi-level LAN segmentation.

---

16 Ethernet hubs are still found in older networks, but they are no longer commercially available and are generally considered to be legacy equipment.

Networks with Bridge Loops and Broadcast Storms

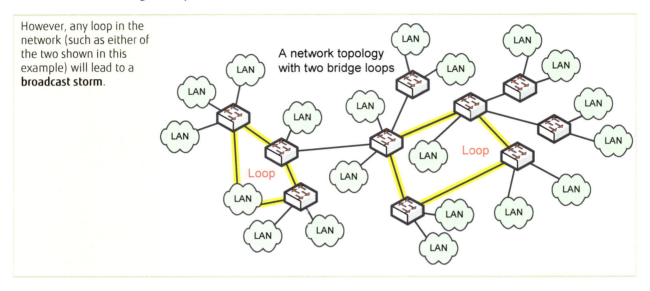

However, any loop in the network (such as either of the two shown in this example) will lead to a **broadcast storm**.

A network topology with two bridge loops

Broadcast storm – a never-ending circulation of broadcast traffic within the network, consuming more and more network resources until part or all of the network can no longer support normal traffic.

A loop produces a broadcast storm as follows:

1. Whenever a bridge/switch receives a broadcast frame (or an unknown unicast frame), it replicates the frame and forwards it to every port, except the one it was received on.

2. If there is a loop in the network, each bridge in the loop does the same thing (replicates and forwards the frame), and the frame goes around and around the loop forever, consuming network resources.

3. Each time a bridge/switch in the loop receives a new broadcast frame (or unknown unicast frame), the same thing happens again, and another frame starts endlessly cycling around the loop, consuming yet more resources.

4. Eventually, all network resources in the loop are used up, and the loop can no longer support normal traffic.

Bridge Loop Prevention and Network Protection

Broadcast storms can be prevented by ensuring that the network topology is free of bridge loops. But ensuring a loop-free network topology can be difficult because simple misconnection of a cable can produce a bridge loop. Furthermore, loop-free networks are undesirable in many applications because they are vulnerable to link failure.

If a single link fails as shown in this example, the network is split into two pieces, making it impossible for many Ethernet end stations to communicate.

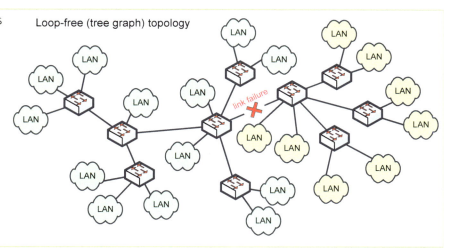

Loop-free (tree graph) topology

For these reasons, the physical topology of real networks is typically not loop-free.

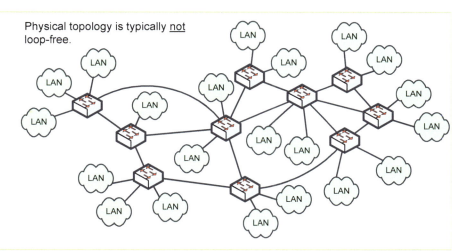

Physical topology is typically not loop-free.

Instead, networks are controlled to operate over loop-free logical topologies (through bridge/switch port blocking).

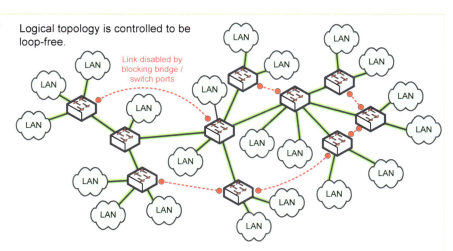

Logical topology is controlled to be loop-free.

The links disabled by port blocking are on standby, ready to be used to fix the network if a link in the active loop-free topology fails.

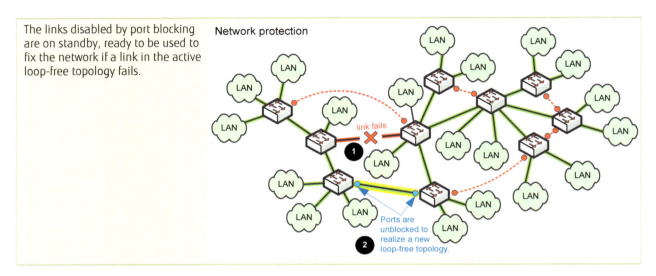

This discussion highlights two very important and highly interrelated issues:

*   **Bridge loop prevention** – Ensuring loop-free topology

*   **Network protection** – Restoring connectivity in the event of link failure

If network protection is not required, bridge loop prevention can be accomplished by careful planning and implementation. Otherwise, these two issues are conventionally resolved using a spanning tree protocol.

Spanning Tree Protocols

Spanning Tree Protocol (STP) – A protocol used by bridges/switches to determine, establish, and maintain a loop-free topology that includes every reachable Ethernet end station in the network.

Rapid Spanning Tree Protocol (RSTP) – An enhancement to STP that provides for faster convergence when there is a change in the physical network topology (for example, due to link failure).

Note: *Every MAC bridge/switch that claims compliance with IEEE 802.1D–2004 must include RSTP capability. Every bridge/switch that claims compliance with IEEE 802.1D–1998 must include STP capability. RSTP is backward compatible with STP.*

Spanning tree protocols enable a network of bridges/switches to automatically configure itself, blocking ports as required, to establish and maintain a loop-free topology that includes every reachable Ethernet end station in the network. The process is distributed: an instance of the process runs on each bridge/switch, and these instances exchange information through messages called BPDUs.

A **BPDU (bridge protocol data unit)** is an Ethernet frame exchanged between bridges/switches to support a spanning tree protocol. Each type of spanning tree protocol (STP, RSTP, or MSTP[17]) defines BPDUs differently, but all BPDUs use the same multicast MAC address.[18]

---

17 **MSTP (Multiple Spanning Tree Protocol)** is yet another form of spanning tree protocol used in VLAN bridging (described later in this book).

Note: *The BPDU is also an example of a* **Layer 2 control protocol (L2CP)** *frame, which is a special category of Ethernet frames that are used for a variety of purposes related to the process of Layer 2 communication, but do not carry data from the perspective of endpoint communication.*

STP and RSTP establish loop-free networks through processes that require no configuration (simple activation in each bridge switch is sufficient to produce a loop-free topology), but can be configured (fine tuned) to guide outcomes.[19]

After establishing a loop-free topology, spanning tree protocols monitor connectivity.[20] Any change in connectivity (loss of connectivity or an addition of new connectivity) can trigger reconfiguration and result in an entirely new loop-free topology. When a spanning tree protocol is converging to a loop-free topology, the network does not support normal traffic. Protection switching performance can be difficult to predict because reconvergence to a new loop-free topology depends on many factors, including network size and complexity.

Related Links

MAC Addresses on p. 25

2.3.4
Summary

MAC bridging allows LANs to grow bigger, compared to shared media LANs, because network congestion is less likely to occur. Bandwidth is no longer shared across the whole network, and a single malfunctioning end station is unlikely to effect the entire network. Congestion can still occur (for example, if multiple end stations try to communicate with the same destination, typically a server, at the same time), but it is much less likely to occur.

However, even with MAC bridging, LAN size is still limited by two issues:

- **Broadcast traffic scaling issue** — Each end station increases the amount of total network bandwidth that is consumed by broadcast, multicast, and unknown unicast traffic. Therefore, a network with too many end stations has little or no bandwidth left to support ordinary, known unicast traffic.

- **Forwarding database size issue** — If the number of end stations in a LAN is significantly greater than the number of MAC addresses that the forwarding database (within a bridge/switch) can hold, the database will fill completely, rendering the bridge/switch unable to learn new MAC addresses. Thereafter, the bridge/switch will flood (broadcast) unicast frames that it should have learned to forward intelligently. Excessive flooding, in turn, consumes bandwidth throughout the LAN, seriously degrading network performance.

Virtual LANs (VLANs), described next, can help mitigate these issues because they constrain broadcast and flooding to be per-VLAN, rather than network-wide.

---

18 Multicast MAC address 01-80-C2-00-00-00 is reserved for BPDUs. Multicast MAC addresses were described earlier in this book.
19 IEEE 802.1D defines STP and RSTP. Many computer networking textbooks include excellent descriptions of STP and RSTP.
20 **Hello BPDUs** are sent at regular intervals. Failure to receive **Hello BPDUs**, as expected, signals a change in topology.

2.4
Virtual LANs

In this section:

VLAN Bridging (IEEE 802.1Q–2005) is similar to MAC Bridging (IEEE 802.1D), but with mechanisms added to support **virtual LANs** (VLANs).

Virtual LAN — Logical LAN connectivity, within a physical LAN, that emulates IEEE 802.1D network connectivity

A LAN, as defined by IEEE 802.1D, includes every Ethernet end station that is physically connected (every Ethernet end station can communicate with every other Ethernet end station).

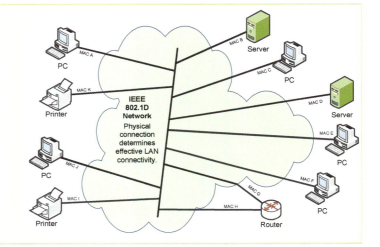

In contrast, a VLAN, as defined by IEEE 802.1Q–2005, includes only a subset of the physically connected Ethernet end stations (to communicate, Ethernet end stations must be members of the same VLAN).

Typically, each Ethernet end station is assigned to one (and only one) VLAN, as shown in the previous figure. However, Ethernet end stations that are VLAN-aware (not typical) can be assigned to more than one VLAN.

Note: *For simplicity, this book assumes that Ethernet end stations are not VLAN-aware.*

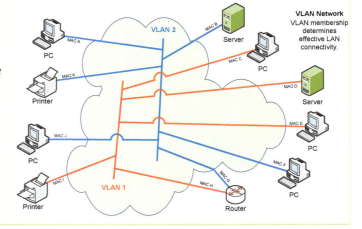

VLANs are very useful in network management because they allow the network manager to determine effective LAN connectivity through software configuration, rather than through physical connections. In an enterprise network, all Ethernet end stations are typically connected to a single physical LAN and assigned to different VLANs, as required (for example, to support different business organizations such as Human Resources, Engineering, and Accounting). VLANs can also improve networking efficiency in very large networks because broadcasting and flooding (of unknown unicast frames) are confined to VLANs.

Note: *The correct current standard for VLAN bridging is IEEE 802.1Q–2011. This book references noncurrent standard IEEE 802.1Q–2005 to avoid any confusion between the original form of VLAN bridging (described in this book) with more advanced forms (Provider Bridging and Provider Backbone Bridging) that are combined with VLAN bridging in IEEE 802.1Q–2011.*

Related Links

About IEEE 802.1Q and VLAN Bridging Terminology on p. 104

2.4.1
VLAN Networks

A **VLAN-aware bridge/ switch** is bridge/switch that complies with IEEE 802.1Q–2005.

A **VLAN network** is an Ethernet network that includes one or more VLAN-aware bridges/ switches and any number of Ethernet end stations.

Each VLAN-aware bridge/ switch can support an arbitrary number of Ethernet end stations. Each Ethernet end station connects to one (and only one) VLAN-aware bridge/ switch. However, that connection can be either direct or indirect (through an ordinary switched or unswitched Ethernet LAN).

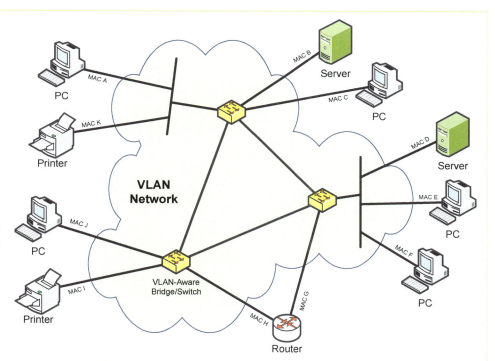

Related Links

Ethernet End Station on p. 21

2.4.2
VLAN Topologies

Each VLAN within the network is supported by a specific topology that is a subset of the overall VLAN network topology.

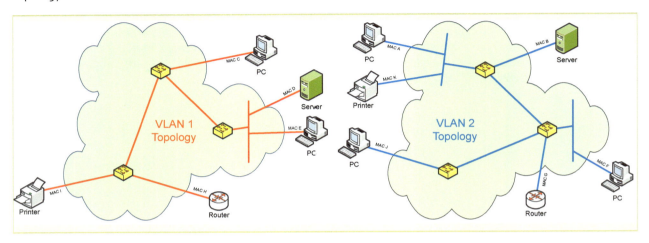

The topology for each VLAN:

1. Connects all of the Ethernet end stations that the VLAN supports.

2. Is loop-free (or is controlled to be loop-free), as previously explained for MAC bridging (to prevent broadcast storms).

Note: *As previously stated, each Ethernet end station typically belongs to only one VLAN. However, an Ethernet end station can belong to more than one VLAN if it is VLAN-aware (not typical).*

Related Links

Bridge Loop Prevention and Network Protection on p. 38

2.4.3
VLAN-Aware Bridging

To emulate IEEE 802.1D MAC bridging within each VLAN, VLAN-aware bridges/switches are configured to perform MAC address learning on a per-VLAN basis and to forward frames on a per-VLAN basis. Each VLAN-aware bridge/switch is configured to:

*   Associate a specific set of ports with each VLAN.

*   Map each received frame[21] onto a single VLAN and forward it appropriately using MAC address learning and forwarding constrained to that VLAN.

---

21 Excluding non-traffic bearing Ethernet frames, such as Layer 2 Control Protocol (L2CP) frames, which are not always mapped to VLANs.

VLAN-aware bridges/ switches support two types of ports:

- **Edge Port** — A port that supports non-VLAN-aware Ethernet end stations is an **edge port** with respect to the VLAN network.

- **Network Port** — A port that connects to another VLAN-aware bridge/switch is a **network port** with respect to the VLAN network.

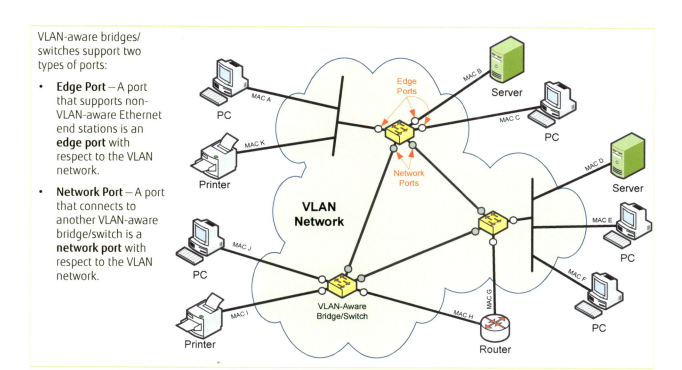

For simplicity, this book assumes that Ethernet end stations are <u>not</u> VLAN-aware (which is typical). At edge ports, Ethernet frames can be untagged or priority tagged.[22] At network ports, all traffic-bearing[23] Ethernet frames include a **VLAN tag** that carries VLAN identification information and some other information, as explained in the next section. The appendix includes a more detailed explanation of VLAN bridging.

Related Links

VLAN Bridging In Detail on p. 98
Priority-Tagged Ethernet Frames on p. 103

2.4.4
Ethernet Frames and VLAN Tags

Per IEEE 802.1Q–2005, Ethernet frames in a VLAN network can be untagged or tagged. An untagged frame conforms to IEEE 802.1D. A tagged frame includes a **VLAN tag** inserted after the source MAC address.

---

22 A **priority-tagged** frame is a tagged Ethernet frame with VID=0. Refer to the appendix for more information.
23 Non-traffic bearing frames, such as Layer 2 Control Protocol (L2CP) frames, may not include a VLAN tag.

The VLAN tag is composed of the following components:

Tag protocol identifier (TPID) — 16 bits with hexadecimal value 8100, which identifies the frame as a tagged frame conforming to the IEEE 802.1Q–2005 standard

Tag control information (TCI) consisting of:

- **Priority code point (PCP)** — 3 bits representing one of eight priority levels (0–7)

- **Canonical format indicator (CFI)** — One bit used for various purposes but not used for Ethernet frames (set to zero)

- **VLAN identifier (VID)** — 12 bits representing one of 4094 values; identifies the VLAN to which the frame belongs

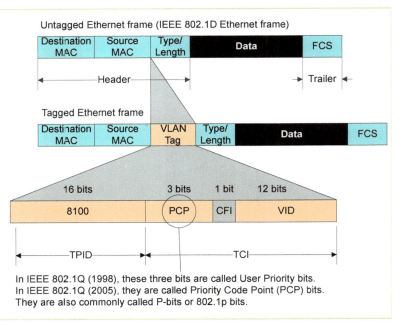

The IEEE 802.1Q–2005 VLAN tag (a VLAN tag with TPID=8100) is now commonly called a **Customer VLAN tag** or **C-Tag** because in Provider Bridging (IEEE 802.1ad) it represents customer-level VLAN tagging. IEEE 802.1ad Provider bridging includes another tag called the service VLAN tag or S-Tag that is used by the service provider.

Related Links

The S-Tag on p. 90
About IEEE 802.1Q and VLAN Bridging Terminology on p. 104

2.4.5
VLAN Bridge Loop Prevention and Network Protection

In VLAN networks, bridge loop prevention and network protection are critical (and highly coupled) issues, just as they are in IEEE 802.1D networks. However, in VLAN networks, these issues can be resolved on a per-VLAN basis using MSTP.

Multiple Spanning Tree Protocol (MSTP) — An extension to RSTP that supports multiple instances of the spanning tree protocol, each running independently and supporting a different group of VLANs.

MSTP is also useful for balancing traffic loads within the network. Because each spanning tree instance runs over a different network topology, they can be engineered to mitigate network congestion.

Related Links

Spanning Tree Protocols on p. 40

2.5

Summary

Ethernet LAN technology has evolved to support larger and larger LANs:

- Early shared media LANs (coaxial cable LANs and hubs LANs) were relatively small due to bandwidth limitations, collisions, and the potential for a single malfunctioning end station to bring down the whole network.

- MAC bridging overcame these problems, allowing much bigger LANs that were now limited by the effect of flooding/broadcast traffic consuming too much of the available network bandwidth (in LANs that have too many end stations).

- VLANs can help mitigate this issue because they constrain flooding and broadcasting to be per-VLAN, rather than network-wide. However, LAN size is still limited, even with VLANs.

Thanks to this evolution, LANs can now support hundreds or even thousands of Ethernet end stations.

To create even larger networks, routers can be used to interconnect LANs. Routers, in effect, partition the network into separate broadcast domains (LANs), each small enough to operate efficiently.

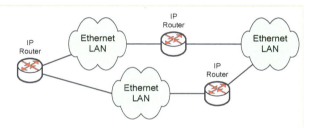

A **broadcast domain** (or **flood domain**) is a logical division of a computer network in which all Ethernet end stations can reach each other through broadcast (or flooding of unknown unicast frames).

The network is no longer purely Ethernet because routers are Layer 3 devices, but computers throughout the network can still communicate:

- If two computers are in the same LAN, they communicate using Ethernet (as described in this chapter).

- If two computers are in different LANs, they communicate using Layer 3 IP (Internet Protocol), but communication at Layer 2 is still by Ethernet.

The appendix includes an explanation of Ethernet used in IP Routing.

As LAN networking became commonplace in the 1980's, many enterprises found themselves with geographically isolated LANs at different sites of operation, which they naturally wanted to interconnect. But distances between sites could be very long, even global.

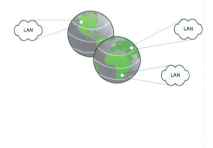

The obvious place to seek such connectivity was through Telecommunications because Telecom networks were very well developed and global in reach. However, Telecom networking technology at that time was exclusively circuit-based, which is profoundly different from packet-based computer networking technology. Understanding this clash of technologies (circuit-based technology versus packet-based technology) is central to understanding Carrier Ethernet.

The next chapter explains traditional circuit-based Telecom technology and how it has been adapted to support Ethernet traffic, allowing the connection of LANs over very long, even global, distances.

Related Links

Ethernet with IP Routing on p. 105

3
Telecom and Carrier Services

In this chapter:

This chapter describes Carrier networking technologies and services prior to Carrier Ethernet.

It includes three sections:

1.   **Traditional TDM-Based Services for Telephone Communication** — Prior to 1980, Carriers (then called Telcos) focused almost exclusively on telephone communication and evolved networks to efficiently support it based on TDM (time division multiplexing) technologies (PDH and SONET/SDH technologies). This section describes the principles of TDM and provides an overview of PDH and SONET/SDH.

2.   **Leased Line Services for Wide Area Networking** — Around 1980, computer networking started to place new demands on Carriers to support computer data for wide area networking. This section describes how TDM-based services (known as leased lines) were adapted to transport computer data and why such solutions are not always cost effective.

3.   **Virtual Circuit-Based Services for Wide Area Networking** — Recognizing that TDM technology is not always efficient in data applications, a variety of virtual circuit-based technologies (such as X.25, Frame Relay, and ATM) emerged to support packet-based communication over carrier networks. This section describes how these technology-specific solutions lowered the cost of data services, but placed new demands on enterprise networking professionals to operate and manage specialized, technology-specific routers.

Carrier Ethernet, described in the next chapter, emerges from this context.

3.1
Traditional TDM-Based Services for Telephone Communication

In this section:

3.1.1   Time Division Multiplexing
3.1.2   TDM Circuits and Services
3.1.3   TDM-Based Telecom Technologies
3.1.4   Synchronization and Protection

Traditional telephone service is fundamentally different from data service in a variety of ways. Most notably, it is focused on one application: delivery of continuous, fixed-bandwidth voice signals, in near real-time (with very small delay), with high fidelity, with high reliability, and over very long distances.

Prior to 1980, Telecom networks used only circuit-based technologies because telephone service (the only service of significant commercial interest at that time) is efficiently carried by circuits. Circuit-based Telecom networking was originally based on analog electrical circuits over copper wire pairs, but now uses digital circuits over a variety of transport media, including over copper wire pairs, fiber-optic cables, and wireless links. A digital circuit is basically a steady stream of bits (1s and 0s) between two points. A standard telephone voice call uses two 64 kbps bit streams (one in each direction), called DSO signals.

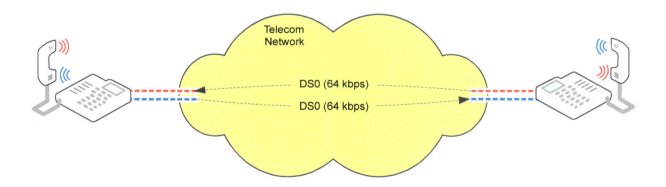

3.1.1
Time Division Multiplexing

Within the Telecom network, an individual link between two **NEs (network elements)** can carry numerous DSO signals (and/or larger signals) through **TDM (time-division multiplexing)** technology. TDM technology comes in many forms, but all work on the principle of interleaving bits from some number of low-speed signals onto one high-speed signal, as shown in the following example.

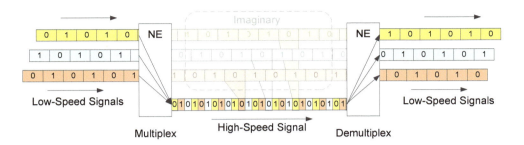

Note: *The process of combining low-speed signals into one high-speed signal is called* **multiplexing**. *The reverse process is called* **demultiplexing**.

In this example, the high-speed signal is formed by interleaving individual bits from the low-speed signals. In practice, **time divisions (fixed-length strings of bits)** are interleaved (not individual bits), but the principle is the same, regardless of the number of bits in a time division.

As shown in the following example, all time divisions within a low-speed signal have to be the same size (contain the same number of bits), but different low-speed signals can have different-sized time divisions (time divisions in the bottom low-speed signal are two times larger than the time divisions in the other two low-speed signals). Each low-speed signal corresponds to a **time slot** (a periodic sequence of time divisions) in the high-speed signal. Time slots occur cyclically in the high-speed signal.

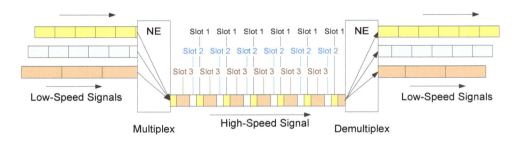

As shown in the following figure, the high-speed signal also includes non-traffic bearing bits called **overhead bits**, which are added for various purposes, including for signal framing and fault/performance management.

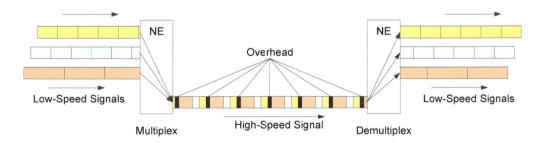

3.1.2
TDM Circuits and Services

Traditional Telecom services are implemented using TDM technology to configure one or more digital circuits through the network. A phone call, for example, is supported by two digital circuits (one in each direction) as shown conceptually in the following figure.

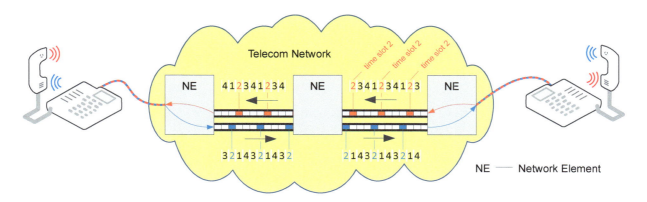

Each circuit, in essence, provides a fixed-bandwidth digital signal between two sites.

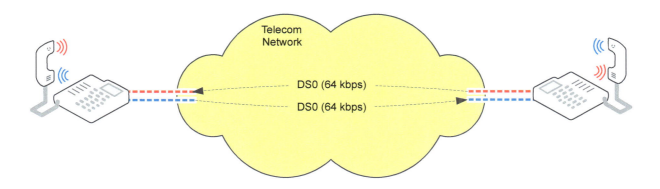

In the case of a telephone call, the circuits are created automatically by switches when the call is placed and removed automatically when the call is ended. But, regardless of how the circuits are created and deleted, all network resources (time slots) supporting the circuits are completely dedicated to the service for the duration of the phone call (or service agreement).

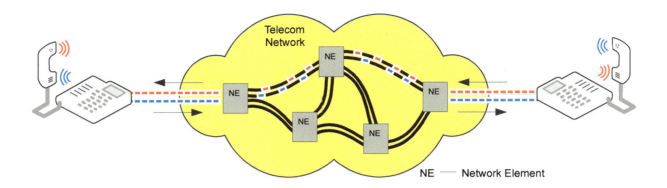

TDM technology, in effect, partitions **line bandwidth** (bandwidth in the link between two NEs) into fixed-bandwidth channels. Circuits through the network are created by connecting these channels, through switching at NEs, as shown conceptually in the following figure.

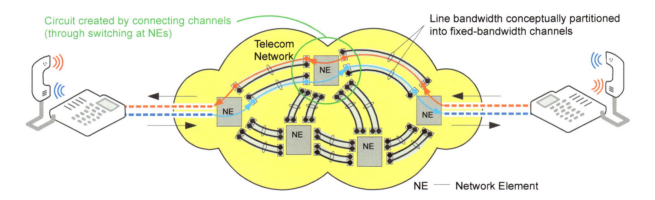

This channelized model of network bandwidth clarifies that each TDM service consumes a very well-defined piece of the overall network bandwidth and that each TDM service provides a fixed-bandwidth circuit through the carrier network for exclusive use by one customer

3.1.3
TDM-Based Telecom Technologies

Four systems of TDM-based technology are used worldwide.

In the United States and Canada:
• **T-Carrier** – Older system designed for electrical transmission media
• **SONET (Synchronous Optical Network)** – Newer system designed for optical transmission media
In the Rest of the Word:
• **E-Carrier** – Older system designed for electrical transmission media
• **SDH (Synchronous Digital Hierarchy)** – Newer system designed for optical transmission media

T-Carrier and E-Carrier are based on PDH (Plesiochronous Digital Hierarchy) technology. SONET and SDH are based on synchronous optical networking technology.

PDH (Plesiochronous Digital Hierarchy)

Although the DS0 signal (64 kbps, supporting one telephone call) is foundational to Telecommunications in general, it is too small to be used within the Telecom industry for network operations or to support applications that require more bandwidth, such as video telecommunications.

PDH (Plesiochronous Digital Hierarchy) is a standardized system of TDM-based Telecom technology that defines a hierarchy of larger signals (anchored by the DS0 signal) and line services (for electrical copper-pair transmission media) based on those signals. There are two systems of PDH technology:

- **T-Carrier** – Used in the US and Canada

- **E-Carrier** – Used in the rest of the world

In each system, two line services are commonly used:

T-Carrier System	Description
T1 line service	Supports one DS1 signal (1.5 Mb/s), which can be used on its own or to support up to 24 DS0 signals (each 64 kb/s).
T3 line service	Supports one DS3 signal (45 Mb/s), which can be used on its own or to support up to 28 DS1 signals (each 1.5 Mb/s). Each DS1 signal, in turn, can be used on its own or to support up to 24 DS0 signals (each 64 kb/s). The T3 line service can support a maximum of 672 DS0 signals.

E-Carrier System	Description
E1 line service	Supports one E1 signal (2.0 Mb/s), which can be used on its own or to support up to 32 DS0 signals (each 64 kb/s).
E3 line service	Supports one E3 signal (34 Mb/s), which can be used on its own or to support up to 16 E1 signals (each 2.0 Mb/s). Each E1 signal, in turn, can be used on its own or to support up to 32 DS0 signals (each 64 kb/s). The E3 line service can support a maximum of 512 DS0 signals.

Line services are configured through a Telecom network by cross connecting digital signals at NEs within the network. Telecos configure line services on request and lease them to customers (other Telecos, businesses, or individuals).

Private telephone networks are created by leasing line services from one or more Telecos and using those line services to connect private branch exchanges (PBXs) that are owned and operated by the customer.

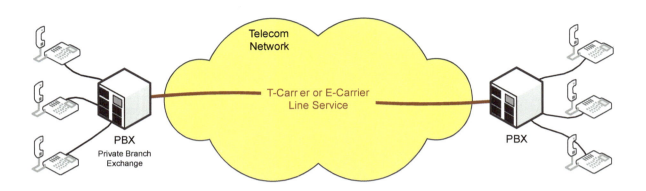

SONET and SDH

SONET (Synchronous Optical Network) and SDH (Synchronous Digital Hierarchy) are standardized systems of TDM-based Telecom technology, each defining a hierarchy of signals, similar to the hierarchy of PDH signals. However, SONET and SDH are more advanced technologies compared to PDH technology, and are designed for optical networks, rather than for copper-pair electrical networks. Compared to PDH, SONET and SDH provide higher performance and larger bandwidths.

SONET and SDH are similar technologies, but are defined by different standards. Both are widely deployed today. SONET is used in the U.S. and Canada. SDH is used in the rest of the world. The following table lists the hierarchy of commonly used SONET and SDH signal levels.

SONET		SDH	Bandwidth	
OC-*n* (Optical)	STS-*n* (Electrical)	STM-*n* (Optical/Electrical)	Payload (Approx.)	Line Rate (Approx.)
OC-1	STS-1	STM-0	50 Mb/s	52 Mb/s
OC-3	STS-3	STM-1	150 Mb/s	155 Mb/s
OC-12	STS-12	STM-4	601 Mb/s	622 Mb/s
OC-48	STS-48	STM-16	2.4 Gb/s	2.5 Gb/s
OC-192	STS-192	STM-64	9.6 Gb/s	10 Gb/s
OC-768	STS-768	STM-256	38.5 Gb/s	40 Gb/s

- Synchronous transport signal (STS-*n*) refers to the SONET signal in the electrical domain.
- Optical carrier (OC-*n*) refers to the SONET signal in the optical domain.
- Synchronous transport module (STM-*n*) refers to the SDH signal level in both domains (electrical and optical).

Similar to PDH signals, SONET/SDH signals are sized hierarchically so that smaller signals fit efficiently inside larger signals with some bandwidth reserved for overhead (the difference between line rate and payload bandwidth). The following table lists the maximum number of electrical signals, per electrical signal level, for each optical carrier level.

Optical Carrier Level	Maximum Number of Electrical Domain Signals					
	STS-1 (STM-0)	STS-3 (STM-1)	STS-12 (STM-4)	STS-48 (STM-16)	STS-192 (STM-64)	STS-768 (STM-256)
OC-1 (STM-0)	1	0	0	0	0	0
OC-3 (STM-1)	3	1	0	0	0	0
OC-12 (STM-4)	12	4	1	0	0	0
OC-48 (STM-16)	48	16	4	1	0	0
OC-192 (STM-64)	192	64	16	4	1	0
OC-768 (STM-256)	768	256	64	16	4	1

The signals are sized hierarchically, like divisions on a ruler:

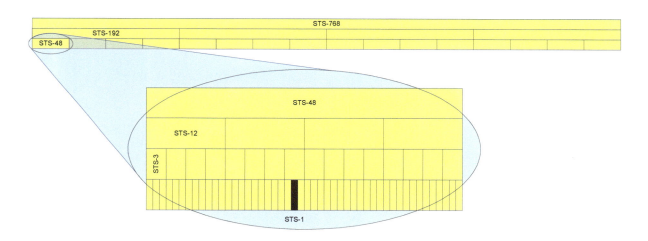

Higher-level signals carry lower-level signals as payload. Higher-level signals can carry a mixture of lower-level signals as shown in the following example.

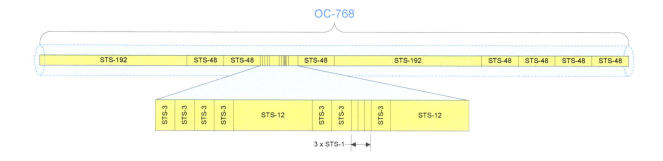

PDH over SONET/SDH

Technologies have been developed that allow PDH and SONET/SDH technologies to interoperate. For example, a SONET STS-1 circuit (which has a payload capacity of about 50 Mb/s) is commonly used to carry 1 DS3 signal (45 Mb/s) or 28 DS1 signals (each 1.5 Mb/s).

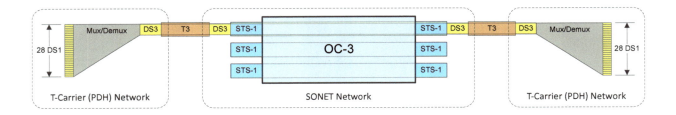

The overall Telecom network consists of an aggregation of PDH networks (local road systems) interconnected with SONET/SDH networks (superhighway systems).

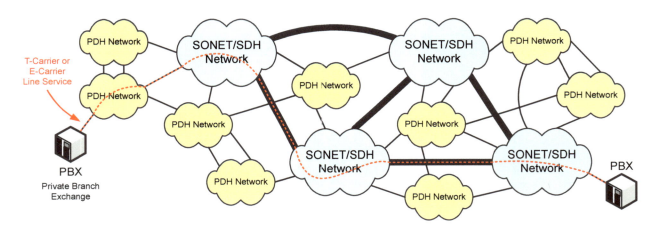

Because both technologies (PDH and SONET/SDH) are TDM-based technologies, services across the aggregate network take the form of fixed-bandwidth circuits. An end-to-end customer service maps onto a fixed-bandwidth circuit through the aggregate Telecom network, and al bandwidth within that circuit is dedicated to a particular service and customer.

3.1.4
Synchronization and Protection

A Telecom service is more than just a continuous, fixed-bandwidth circuit through the network. The circuit must be able to deliver a voice signal in near real-time (with very small delay), with high fidelity, and do it very reliably over long distances.

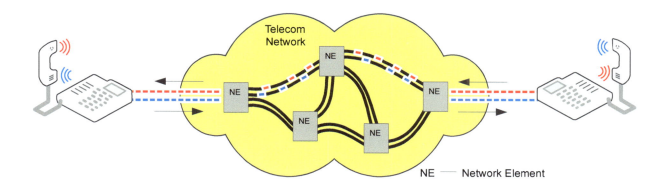

Prior to optical networking, a small delay was sometimes noticeable in long-distance telephone connections. However, with current speed-of-light transport technology, delay is now typically imperceptible to humans, even over very-long-distance (even international) telephone calls.

Synchronization

As bits move through a TDM circuit, they are handed off at NEs (through digital switching) from one TDM signal to another. If the TDM signals are not frequency synchronized, valid bits can be lost and/or invalid bits can be inserted during the handoff. If the circuit includes many NEs, the voice signal is subject to numerous handoffs, each of which can corrupt the signal. For this reason, synchronization, in some form, is vital to all TDM-based Telecom technologies:

- Plesiochronous Digital Hierarchy (PDH)

- Synchronous Optical Network (SONET)

- Synchronous Digital Hierarchy (SDH)

SONET and SDH ensure frequency synchronization by ensuring that all NEs in the network are synchronized to a single common clock source. PDH allows NEs to be plesiochronous (almost, but not quite, perfectly synchronized) and employs a system to cope with so-called "sync slips" that occur predictably due to the plesiochronous nature of the system.

Availability

Availability refers to the percentage of time that a service is available (not down). In the Telecom industry, the common standard for availability is 99.999% (so-called **Five 9s availability**), which means the total downtime over an entire year is about 5 minutes or less. To achieve this standard, Telecoms employ a variety of protection mechanisms.

Service Protection

Service protection mechanisms keep the service operating even when certain types of failures occur. Service protection can involve a variety of protection mechanisms, but each involves some kind of redundant functionality, fault detection, and protection switching. The common standard for protection switching in the Telecom industry allows up to **50 milliseconds** for fault detection and recovery. Two common forms of protection are **1+1 Linear Protection** and **1:1 Linear Protection**.

1+1 Linear Protection

For clarity, only one direction of service traffic is shown.

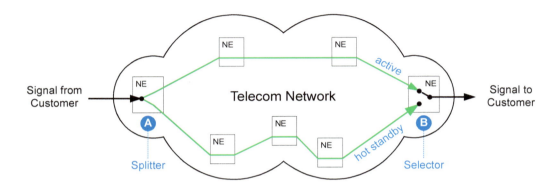

Unidirectional traffic from A to B is protected as follows:

1. At A, the received customer signal is duplicated and sent to B along two distinct network paths.

2. Two copies of the signal are received at B.

3. At B, one of the two copies is selected for transmission.

4. Failure in the active signal is detected at B and triggers switching.

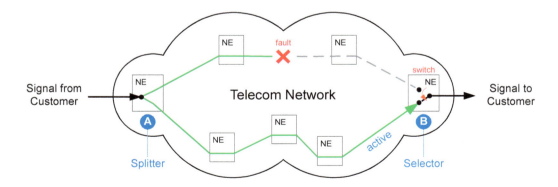

To protect bidirectional traffic, this scheme is used in both directions.

Unidirectional path-switched ring (UPSR) protection is an example of a 1+1 linear protection technology.

1:1 Linear Protection

For clarity, only one direction of service traffic is shown.

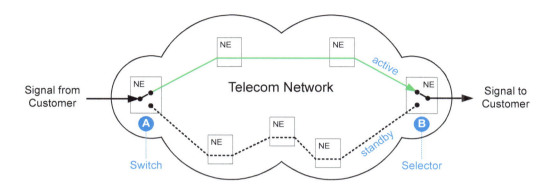

Unidirectional traffic from A to B is protected as follows:

1. Two distinct network paths from A to B are provisioned: a working path and a protect path.

2. In normal operation, the working path is active. The protect path is on standby.

3. Failure in the active signal is detected at B and triggers protection switching at two locations (A and B) to deactivate the working path and activate the standby path.

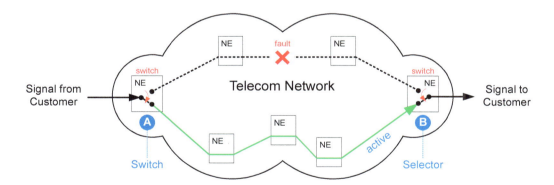

Note: *To trigger switching at A, a failure signal is sent from B to A through a reverse-direction path that, for simplicity, is not shown in the figures.*

Because the standby path does not carry replicated traffic, it can potentially carry other traffic.

To protect bidirectional traffic, this scheme is used in both directions.

Bidirectional line-switched ring (BLSR) protection is an example of a 1:1 linear protection technology.

3.2
Leased Line Services for Wide Area Networking

In this section:

3.2.1   Multipoint WAN Connectivity
3.2.2   TDM Network Bandwidth Utilization

As LAN networking became commonplace in the 1980's, many enterprises found themselves with geographically isolated LANs at different sites of operation, which they naturally wanted to interconnect. But distances between sites could be very long, even global. The obvious place to seek such **WAN (wide area networking)** connectivity was through Telecom networks, which were very well developed and global in reach.

Leased line services (T-Carrier / E-Carrier services) were readily available (used for PBX interconnection), and enterprises began using them, typically with routers, to interconnect LANs as shown.

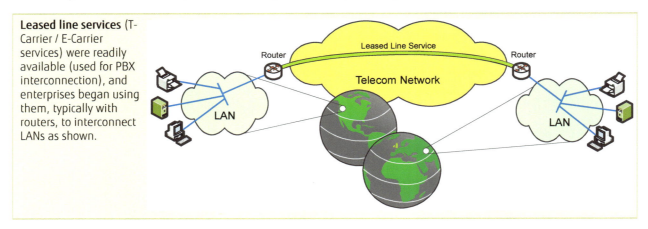

Adaptation of leased line services to Ethernet WAN applications involves three fundamental challenges:

- **Data Encapsulation** — How to encode Ethernet frames (or the data within Ethernet frames) into the leased line service payload (before transmission) and how to decode (or rebuild) Ethernet frames from the leased line service payload (after transmission).

- **Traffic Management** — How to funnel bursty LAN traffic from a high-bandwidth Ethernet interface into a much smaller-bandwidth leased line interface.[24] For example, traffic from a 10 Mb/s, or a 100 Mb/s, Ethernet interface might be channeled into a T1 leased line (with 1.5 Mb/s payload) or into a T3 leased line (with 45 Mb/s payload).

- **Multipoint Connectivity** — How to accomplish any-to-any connectivity (when more than two enterprise locations are involved).

For practical reasons, commercial equipment manufacturers have adapted routers (not Ethernet switches) to meet these challenges. Such routers include Ethernet interfaces, leased-line interfaces, and queueing[25] features to support traffic management.

---

24 The cost of leased line service bandwidth drives its minimization in WAN applications.
25 Queuing features can help to mitigate traffic management issues, through buffering, prioritizing, scheduling, and by judiciously dropping (low-priority) traffic, and they can help pack more traffic onto the leased line service when inter-LAN traffic bursts beyond the leased line service bandwidth. However, they cannot ensure that the leased line service bandwidth is well utilized (when there is no inter-LAN traffic, line service bandwidth is unused) or necessarily ensure that all inter-LAN traffic is delivered.

3.2.1
Multipoint WAN Connectivity

If an enterprise requires any-to-any connectivity between three or more LAN locations, it can be accomplished using leased lines (and in more than one way). In the extreme, the enterprise can purchase a full mesh of leased line services to interconnect enterprise locations as shown in this example.

But this is rarely done because each leased line service is costly.

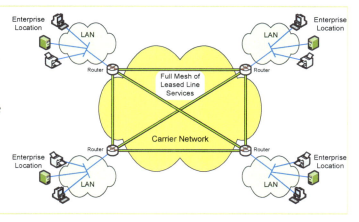

Enterprises typically deploy a partial mesh of leased lines, often only a hub-and-spoke topology of leased lines as shown in this example. Hub-and-spoke topology is commonly used because in many applications one site (the enterprise headquarters, for example) is a natural hub (the known focus of most WAN traffic).

Partial mesh topologies still support any-to-any connectivity. But they support it less directly (than the full-mesh topology) because traffic between some LANs have to traverse more than one leased line.

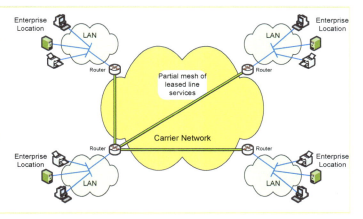

Because leased line services are implemented with dedicated TDM circuits provisioned through the carrier network, they behave very much like purpose-built network links.

Advantages: In some ways, the leased line WAN solution is very attractive. It uses existing, well-developed, and widely deployed Telecom networking technology. It is easy to understand and manage from the enterprise perspective. It provides highly reliable high-performance connectivity very much like a purpose-built network link.

Disadvantages: However, leased lines are costly in WAN applications because they tie up carrier network bandwidth in dedicated circuits that tend to be underutilized due to the sporadic nature of inter-LAN traffic. The enterprise continually pays for (leases) the bandwidth that is consumed by the leased line in the carrier network, regardless of how much traffic actually flows over it. Additionally, the leased line WAN solution is not vary scalable [26] because the number of leased lines (and router ports) that are required can grow very quickly with additional sites (especially in full-mesh applications).

---

[26] Here, the term **scalable** refers to the solution's ability to be enlarged to accommodate growth. The solution is not scalable because the number of leased lines grows very quickly with additional sites, making it impractical to connect more than a few sites. Full mesh multipoint connection of N sites requires $N \times (N-1)/2$ leased lines.

3.2.2
TDM Network Bandwidth Utilization

From the carrier perspective, network bandwidth is the key resource (ever limited by network infrastructure) that is traded (in the form of services) to customers in exchange for money. Making efficient use of network bandwidth is key to offering low-cost services and competing in the marketplace.

Conveyor Belt Model for Link or TDM Circuit Bandwidth

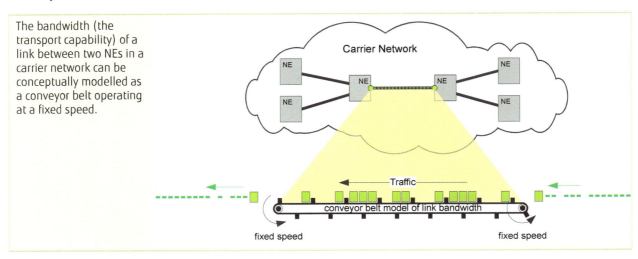

The bandwidth (the transport capability) of a link between two NEs in a carrier network can be conceptually modelled as a conveyor belt operating at a fixed speed.

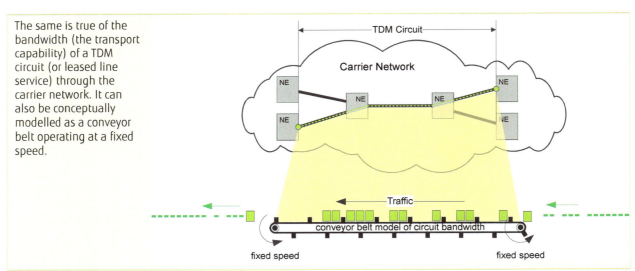

The same is true of the bandwidth (the transport capability) of a TDM circuit (or leased line service) through the carrier network. It can also be conceptually modelled as a conveyor belt operating at a fixed speed.

Note: *The circuit or link is assumed to be unidirectional. If circuit or link is bidirectional, it can be modelled by two conveyor belts, one operating in each direction.*

In this model, conveyor belt speed represents payload bandwidth (for example, 64 kbps to support a standard voice channel, or about 1.5 Mb/s for a T1 leased line). Conveyor belt speed (payload bandwidth) limits how much traffic the circuit or link can support. Actual traffic can be less than payload bandwidth.

TDM Circuit Bandwidth Utilization

In a telephone service application, the TDM circuit is sized (the conveyor belt speed is chosen) to match the steady stream of voice traffic that the telephone service supports. In this case, the circuit cannot support any more traffic. It is fully utilized.

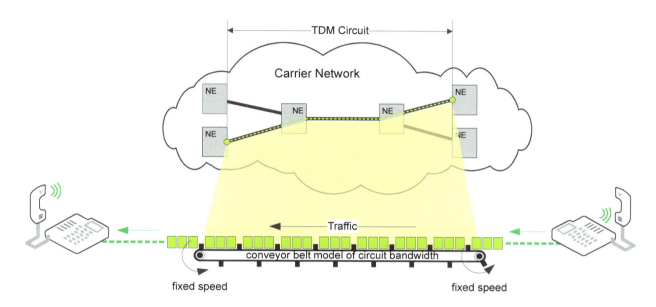

In a data service application, the TDM circuit is sized (the conveyor belt speed is chosen) to match the maximum traffic rate that the service is expected to support. In this case, actual traffic will generally be less than what the circuit can support (due to the sporadic nature of computer data traffic, the circuit bandwidth is larger than the nominal traffic bandwidth).

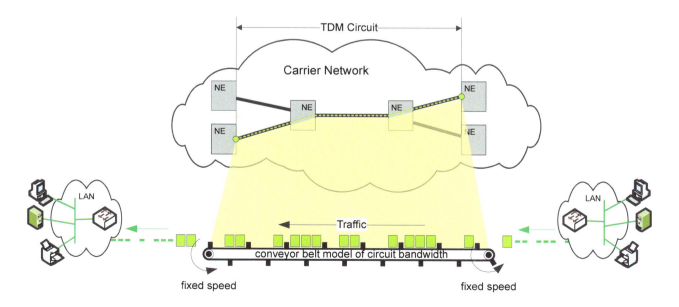

Link Bandwidth Utilization

Now consider a link between two NEs, and for simplicity assume that its total bandwidth is consumed by just two TDM circuits. TDM technology channelizes the total link bandwidth into two independent channels (two time slots), each dedicated to one of the two TDM circuits.

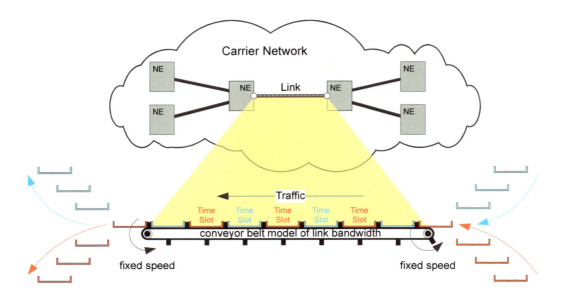

If both TDM circuits carry phone traffic, the link bandwidth is fully utilized.

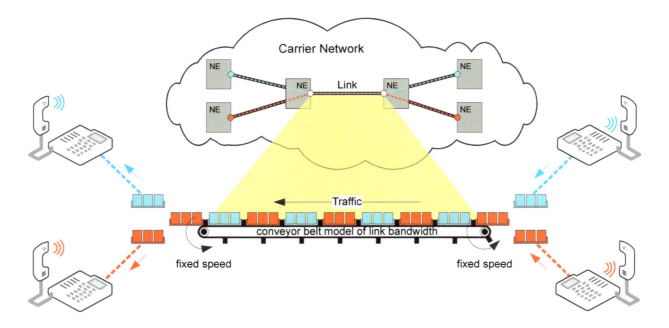

However, if either one or both of the TDM circuits carry data traffic, the link bandwidth will tend to be underutilized.

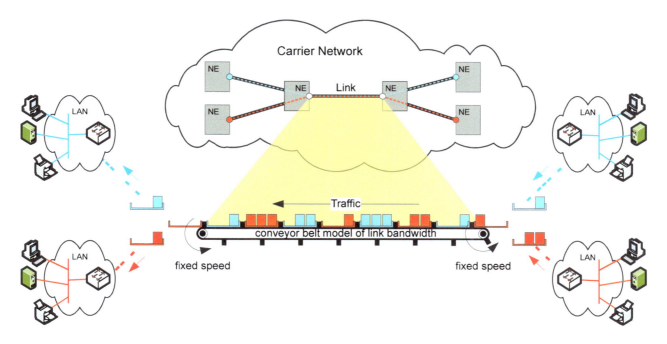

Furthermore, traffic on each TDM circuit is limited by the TDM circuit bandwidth, regardless of the link bandwidth or its current utilization. In the following figure, the red TDM-circuit can carry no more traffic, even though the link currently has spare capacity.

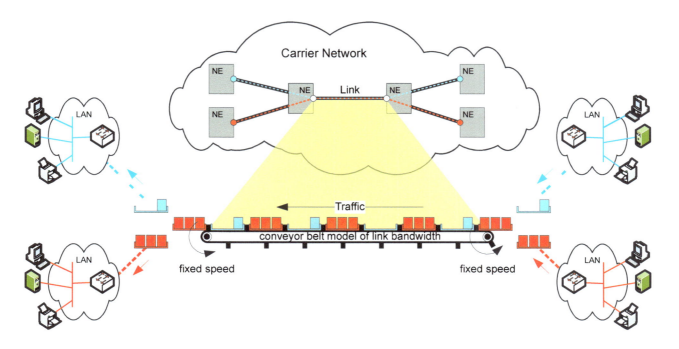

3.3
Virtual Circuit-Based Services for Wide Area Networking

In this section:

Now imagine a different form of carrier networking that does not use TDM technology. Instead the network uses a technology that allows services to truly share link bandwidth as shown in the following example.

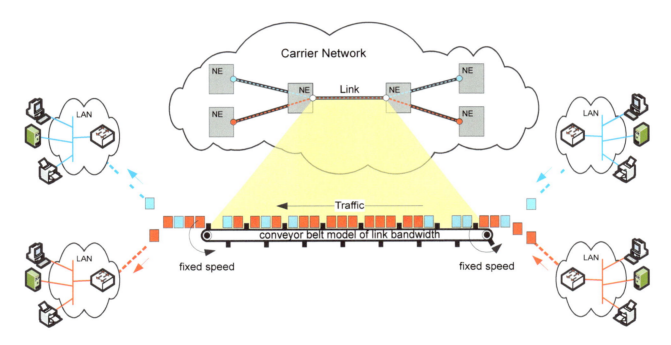

In this example, link bandwidth is shared by two streams of service traffic, and both streams have access to all of the link bandwidth. New traffic management problems arise because both streams now compete for one resource (the total link bandwidth). However, from the carrier perspective, this kind of technology allows link bandwidth throughout the network to be used more efficiently.

3.3.1
Virtual Circuit

A **virtual circuit**[27] is a packet-based connection through the carrier network. A virtual circuit is similar to a TDM circuit (or a leased line service) in that it provides point-to-point connectivity over a predefined network path. However, unlike a TDM circuit (or a leased line service), a virtual circuit is defined by service agreement, rather than by dedicated network resources.

---

27   The term **virtual circuit** is synonymous with **virtual connection** and **virtual channel**.

TDM circuits (and leased line services) provide constant bit rate connectivity with fixed latency[28] through the carrier network. However, bit rate and latency for virtual circuits may vary due to factors such as varying bit rate in the service traffic and/or traffic congestion in the carrier network (due to other customers sharing the same network resources).

Bandwidth for a virtual circuit is defined in the service agreement (between the carrier and the customer) using mechanisms that in effect guarantee that the virtual circuit will support a minimum bit rate and also allow traffic to burst beyond that bit rate (up to well-defined limits).

Latency in a virtual circuit is likewise defined in the service agreement using mechanisms that are similarly more flexible.

3.3.2
Virtual Circuit-Based WAN Technologies (X.25, Frame Relay, and ATM)

Prior to Carrier Ethernet, a variety of virtual circuit-based technologies were developed to support WAN connectivity across carrier networks, including X.25, Frame Relay, and ATM.

These WAN solutions naturally require technology-specific equipment to be deployed in the carrier network.

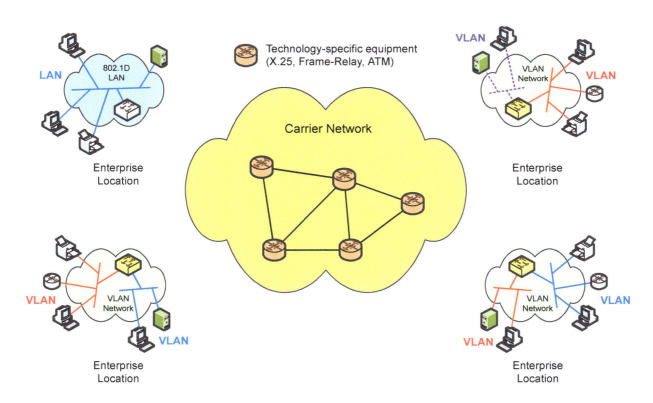

However, they also require technology-specific equipment to be deployed in the to-be-connected enterprise networks.

---

28   **Latency**, a synonym for delay, refers to the time it takes for a packet of data to get from one point to another.

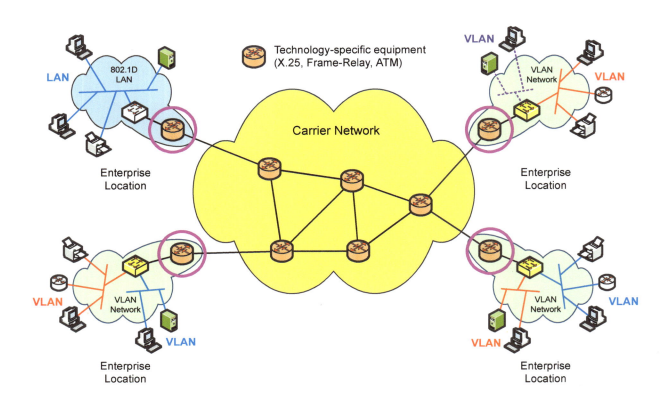

From the enterprise perspective, such solutions can be problematic because they require the enterprise networking professionals to learn and understand a new and unfamiliar technology in order to provision and maintain the new technology-specific devices that now reside in their local networks.

However, compared to the leased-line solution, these solutions are less costly (as carrier services) and more scalable:

- **Cost** — They are less costly because virtual circuits consume network bandwidth less wastefully than TDM circuits. The carrier does not provide fixed bit rate TDM circuits for exclusive use by individual customers (leased lines). Instead, the carrier offers virtual circuits that share network bandwidth more like cars share a public road system. Data from many services and customers (packetized in Layer 2 frames[29]) mix within the carrier network like cars on a highway. Virtual circuits are less costly because they, in effect, provide access to a shared road system, instead of exclusive use of a particular road within the system.

- **Scalability** — Because these solutions are based on Layer 2 technology, each enterprise site can connect to the carrier network through a single port, regardless of how many sites participate in the WAN.

Multipoint functionality (any-to-any connectivity) between sites is supported through a combination of technology-specific virtual circuits (purchased from the carrier) and enterprise-level provisioning of the technology-specific devices that now reside in the local networks.

---

29 Here, Layer 2 frame does not imply Layer 2 <u>Ethernet</u> frame. Technologies such as X.25, Frame Relay, and ATM are other forms of Layer 2 technology.

3.3.3
Frame Relay Example

Suppose the enterprise requires any-to-any WAN connectivity between four locations and the carrier offers Frame Relay services to support it. The enterprise purchases an appropriate number of PVCs (permanent virtual circuits)[30] from the carrier. For example the enterprise might purchase a full mesh of 6 PVCs as shown in the following figure.

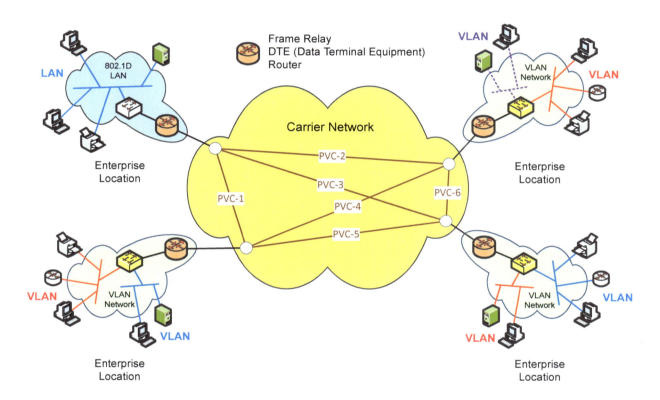

Additionally, to achieve the desired WAN connectivity, the enterprise's own networking professionals have to provision the Frame Relay equipment (DTE routers) that resides in their own networks to associate Ethernet frames appropriately to PVCs.[31]

The solution looks similar to the leased-line solution because leased lines and PVCs are both point-to-point. However, a PVC is much less expensive than a leased line because it is only a virtual circuit through the carrier network, not a real circuit through the network (dedicated to, and exclusively used by, one customer). Of course, this savings comes with the hidden cost of increasing the expertise required within the enterprise's networking group and their workload.

---

30 PVCs are point-to-point virtual connections between sites that Frame Relay subscribers purchase as needed.
31 DTE routers insert a Frame Relay header into each frame, and that header includes a DLCI (data link connection identifier) that binds the service frame to a PVC. Frame relay equipment in the carrier network, called DCE (data communications equipment), then switches frames to PVCs based on the DLCI value.

3.4
Summary

We now understand traditional TDM-based Telecom technology, why it supports circuit-based services very efficiently, and why it tends to support data services less efficiently.

Leased line services (T-Carrier, E-Carrier, SONET, and SDH services), developed for telecommunications, can be adapted (repurposed) for WAN applications. But, in WAN applications, leased line services tend to waste network bandwidth and are consequently expensive to use. Additionally, leased lines require the enterprise (not the carrier) to deal with key WAN connectivity issues, including:

- **Data Encapsulation** – How to encode Ethernet frames (or the data within Ethernet frames) into the leased line service payload (before transmission) and how to decode (or rebuild) Ethernet frames from the leased line service payload (after transmission).

- **Traffic Management** – How to funnel bursty LAN traffic from a high-bandwidth Ethernet interface into a much smaller-bandwidth leased line interface.

- **Multipoint Connectivity** – How to accomplish any-to-any connectivity (when more than two enterprise locations are involved).

Virtual circuit-based technologies, such as X.25, Frame Relay, and ATM, defined at Layer 2, have helped carriers to take a major step toward fully embracing enterprise-perspective WAN requirements. They have improved carrier network bandwidth utilization, driven down the cost of point-to-point WAN services, and allowed multiple services to share the same customer-to-carrier interface.

However, virtual circuit-based WAN solutions still burden the enterprise customer with significant responsibilities that might be migrated to the carrier service. Key ideas for unburdening the enterprise include:

- Remove technology-specific WAN equipment from the enterprise network.

- Define carrier services that migrate more responsibility for WAN connectivity issues to the carrier.

Carrier Ethernet services (described in the next chapter) do not require technology-specific WAN equipment in the enterprise network and migrate key WAN connectivity issues to the carrier as follows:

- **Data Encapsulation** – Carrier Ethernet services are defined between IEEE 802.3 physical Ethernet interfaces, eliminating issues of data encapsulation in the enterprise domain.

- **Traffic Management** – Carrier Ethernet services are defined with bandwidth profiles that, in effect, migrate traffic management issues to the carrier domain.

- **Multipoint Connectivity** – Carrier Ethernet includes multipoint Carrier Ethernet services that, if used, migrate multipoint connectivity issues to the carrier domain.

Carrier Ethernet services are defined in the abstract (independent of whatever technology is used to implement them in the carrier network).

4
Carrier Ethernet Services

In this chapter:

The previous chapters motivate and set the stage for learning about Carrier Ethernet. This chapter provides a broad overview of Carrier Ethernet, highlighting basic terminology, concepts, and the scope of material involved in defining Carrier Ethernet services.

The chapter begins by explaining Carrier Ethernet service terminology and concepts in a simple context (over one carrier network), including:

• **Service Connectivity** – What is connected? What is delivered? To where is it delivered?

• **Traffic Management** – How much traffic is supported? What are the delivery and performance commitments?

• **Operations, Administration, and Management** – What mechanisms are included for fault detection, troubleshooting, and performance monitoring?

The chapter ends with an overview of the MEF framework for implementing Carrier Ethernet services over multiple carrier networks.

The main purpose of this chapter to give you a taste of Carrier Ethernet and a basic framework to help you begin the study of Carrier Ethernet in detail.

4.1
Basic Reference Model

The business model for MEF-defined Carrier Ethernet services involves two principle stakeholders:

- **Subscriber** — The organization purchasing the Carrier Ethernet service

- **Service Provider** — The organization providing the Carrier Ethernet service

In general terms, a Carrier Ethernet service is an Ethernet connection between two or more sites. The sites belong to the subscriber. The network connecting the sites belongs to the service provider.

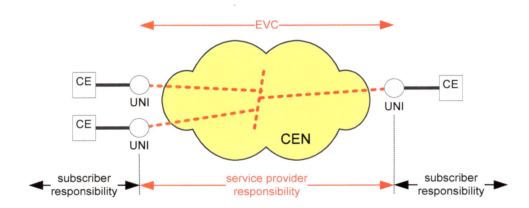

The basic reference model includes the following components:

- **CEN**[32] (Carrier Ethernet Network) — The service provider network used to transport Carrier Ethernet services

- **CE** (Customer Edge Equipment) — The equipment at the subscriber site that connects to the CEN

- **UNI** (User-to-Network Interface) — A physical demarcation point between the subscriber and the service provider

- **EVC** (Ethernet Virtual Connection) — The logical representation of a service connection between two or more UNIs

This *basic reference model* is sufficient for defining Carrier Ethernet services from the subscriber perspective and if only one carrier network is involved. The MEF also defines a *general reference model* (described latter in this chapter) that used if more than one carrier network is involved.

Related Links

General Reference Model on p. 86

---

32 Early MEF specifications use the term MEN (Metro Ethernet Network) in place of CEN. CEN and MEN mean the same thing.

4.2
Service Frames

The MEF defines a **service frame** as an Ethernet frame transmitted across the UNI in either direction (from the subscriber to the service provider or from the service provider to the subscriber).

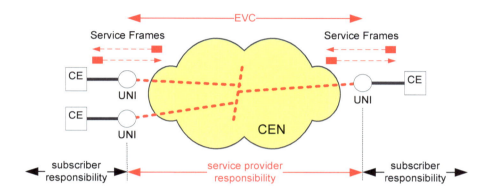

All service frames are either untagged or include a single C-Tag (customer VLAN tag) in the Ethernet header as shown in the following figure.[33]

> Originally, the C-Tag was simply called the *VLAN tag* (per IEEE 802.1Q–2005). It is the same tag as the VLAN tag described earlier in this book when Virtual LANs were described.

Untagged Ethernet frame

Destination MAC	Source MAC	Type/Length	Payload	FCS

The VLAN identifier (VID) includes 12 bits representing one of 4094 values that are used to identify the VLAN to which the Ethernet frame belongs. (Although 12 bits permit 4096 values, two values, 0 and FFF, are reserved for other uses)

C-Tagged Ethernet frame

Destination MAC	Source MAC	C-Tag	Type/Length	Payload	FCS

Drop Eligibility Indicator (DEI)

16 bits	3 bits	1 bit	12 bits
8100	PCP	DEI	VID

TPID — TCI

> Prior to IEEE 802.1Q (2011), the DEI bit was called the Canonical Format Indicator (CFI) bit and was used for a different purpose.

TPID=8100 indicates that this tag is a C-Tag

Since IEEE 802.1Q (1998), these three bits are called User Priority bits. In IEEE 802.1Q (2005), they were called PCP bits. They are also commonly called P-bits, or 802.1p bits.

---

33 This statement is no longer perfectly accurate because, with publication of MEF 10.3, the service frame definition has been extended to accommodate all IEEE 802.3 (2012) Ethernet frame formats (including S-Tagged and I-Tagged Ethernet frames, which are truly atypical). Nevertheless, service frames are still almost always understood to be untagged or C-tagged.

MEF standards recognize two types of C-Tagged service frames: **VLAN-Tagged Service Frames**: (C-Tagged service frames with VID≠0) and **Prority-Tagged Service Frames** (C-Tagged service frames with VID=0). The MEF also recognizes three categories of service frames (independent of tagging):

Data Service Frames

Data service frames support end user applications and are further classified as follows:

- **Unicast Data Service Frames** – Data service frames with a unicast MAC address

- **Multicast Data Service Frames** – Data service frames with a multicast MAC address

- **Broadcast Data Service Frames** – Data service frames with a broadcast MAC address (FF-FF-FF-FF-FF-FF)

Note: Unicast, multicast, and broadcast destination MAC addresses were explained earlier in this book.

L2CP Service Frames

L2CP service frames support Layer 2 Control Protocols, such as STP/RSTP or Link OAM, which are used for network control purposes. They do not carry data from the perspective of endpoint communication. They support networking operations and often require special treatment.

Note: The bridge protocol data unit (BPDU) used by spanning tree protocols (STP and/or RSTP) for bridge loop prevention and network protection is an example of an L2CP frame. There are many other types of L2CP frames used for other purposes.

Carrier Ethernet services handle L2CP service frames on a case-by-case (per protocol) basis. Details of L2CP frame handling are beyond the scope of this introductory book.

SOAM Service Frames

SOAM service frames support Service OAM (Operations, administration, and maintenance) which is used to manage the Carrier Ethernet service (connectivity fault management and performance management).

*Note: Service frames are classified into these categories based on the following logic. If the service frame's destination MAC address corresponds to a Layer 2 Control Protocol[34], it is classified as an **L2CP Service Frame**. Otherwise, if the service frame has Ethertype = 0x8902, it is classified as a **SOAM Service Frame**. Otherwise, the service frame is classified as a **Data Service Frame**.*

Related Links

Ethernet Frames and VLAN Tags on p. 45
Priority-Tagged Ethernet Frames on p. 103
MAC Addresses on p. 25
Spanning Tree Protocols on p. 40
Operations, Administration and Management (OAM) on p. 85

---

34 *IEEE 802.1Q-2011 reserves two blocks of destination MAC address for use by Layer 2 Control Protocols: the Bridge block of addresses (01-80-C2-00-00-00 through 01-80-C2-00-00-0F) and the MRP block of addresses (01-80-C2-00-00-20 through 01-80-C2-00-00-2F).*

4.3
Service Connectivity

In this section:

The MEF defines three types of EVCs: **point-to-point**, **multipoint-to-multipoint**, and **rooted-multipoint**.[35] EVC type determines a variety of service requirements, most notably: how many UNIs the service might connect and conditions (if any) for the delivery of *data service frames* between UNIs.

4.3.1
Point-to-Point EVC

The **point-to-point EVC** connects two UNIs and delivers data frames unconditionally.

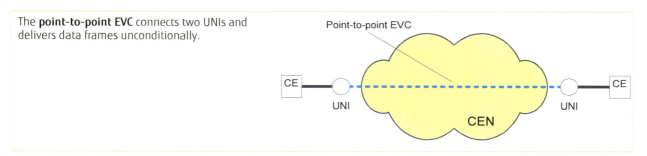

4.3.2
Multipoint-to-Multipoint EVC

The **multipoint-to-multipoint EVC** connects two or more UNIs and allows data frames to be delivered unconditionally or conditionally:

- **Unconditional Delivery**—The EVC delivers data frames to all other UNIs (excluding the ingress UNI) unconditionally, in effect broadcasting Ethernet frames like an Ethernet hub.

- **Conditional Delivery**—The EVC delivers data frames to other UNIs (excluding the ingress UNI) conditionally, <u>per any set of conditions specified in the service agreement</u>.

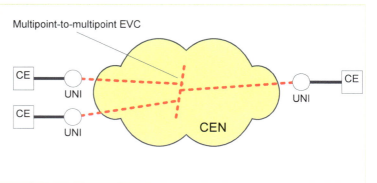

---

35 The MEF also uses the term **multipoint EVC**, but not to define another type of EVC. A **multipoint EVC** is an EVC that is either a multipoint-to-multipoint EVC or a rooted-multipoint EVC.

Conditional versus Unconditional Delivery

Because MEF standards do not define the *conditions* for *conditional delivery*, it is tempting to think that *conditional delivery* is included as an option for handling special (exceptional) cases. However, in practice, conditional delivery is typical, and the conditions for delivery are nearly always specified to produce bridging behavior (MAC address–based learning and frame forwarding) in the EVC. Thus, in practice, **multipoint-to-multipoint** is commonly understood to imply **bridging behavior** because that is how multipoint-to-multipoint EVCs are typically defined. However, multipoint-to-multipoint does not in fact imply bridging behavior. Bridging is a valid form of conditional delivery, but other forms of conditional delivery are equally valid, as well as unconditional delivery.

4.3.3
Rooted-Multipoint EVC

The **rooted-multipoint EVC** connects two or more UNIs and can be configured to deliver data frames just like a multipoint-to-multipoint EVC: unconditionally or conditionally per specified conditions (which in practice typically equate to bridging). However, unlike the multipoint-to-multipoint EVC, the rooted-multipoint EVC prevents some UNIs from forwarding Ethernet frames to other UNIs. Each UNI is declared to be either a **root** or a **leaf**.

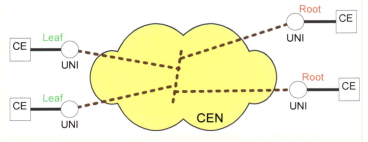

Roots are allowed to forward Ethernet frames to leaves and roots. Leaves can only forward Ethernet frames to roots.

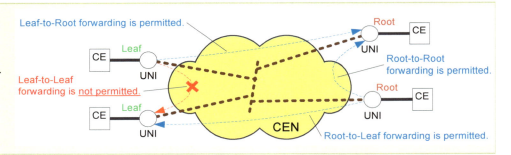

4.3.4
Service Multiplexing

Service multiplexing occurs when a UNI supports more than one EVC. In the following figure, service multiplexing is shown at two of the four UNIs.

Notice that service multiplexing is a property of a UNI. It is not a property of the Ethernet service or EVC.

The key benefit of service multiplexing is that it allows services to share UNIs, saving ports (physical connections) on subscriber and service provider edge equipment.

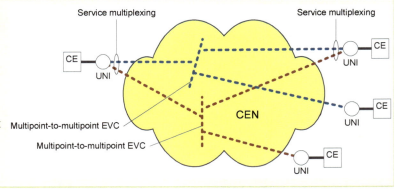

4.3.5
Three Forms of UNI-to-EVC Connectivity

For each type of EVC (point-to-point, multipoint-to-multipoint, and rooted-multipoint), MEF standards allow three forms of UNI-to-EVC connectivity:

Port-based — All service frames present at the UNI map to the EVC.

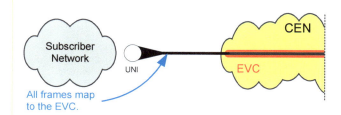

One-channel — A single value of VLAN ID is specified at the UNI. Service frames with that value of VLAN ID map to the EVC.

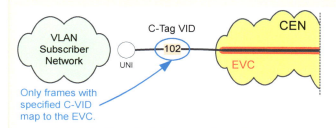

Multi-channel — A set of VLAN ID values is specified at the UNI. Service frames with VLAN ID in that set map to the EVC.

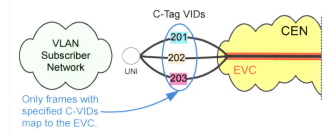

At each UNI of an EVC, the same form of connectivity (port-based, one-channel, or multi-channel) is required. An EVC cannot include a mixture of different connectivities.

 Caution: *The terms **port-based**, **one-channel**, and **multi-channel** are not MEF terms. They are used informally in this book to convey concepts a little more directly and simply than proper MEF terminology allows. In MEF specifications, these three forms of connectivity emerge from the definition of service attributes (**All-to-One Bundling**, **Bundling**, **CE-VLAN ID / EVC Map** and **CE-VLAN ID Preservation**) and requirements for their configuration.*

4.3.6
VLAN ID Translation

VLAN ID translation is only supported if UNI-to-EVC connectivity is single-channel:

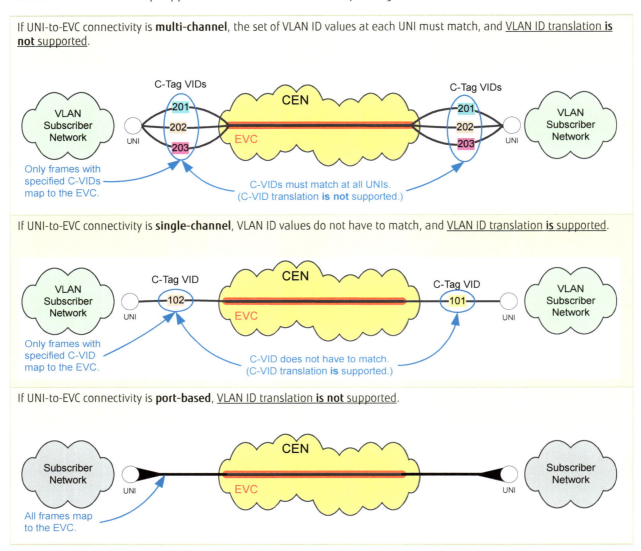

If UNI-to-EVC connectivity is **multi-channel**, the set of VLAN ID values at each UNI must match, and <u>VLAN ID translation **is not** supported</u>.

Only frames with specified C-VIDs map to the EVC.

C-VIDs must match at all UNIs.
(C-VID translation **is not** supported.)

If UNI-to-EVC connectivity is **single-channel**, VLAN ID values do not have to match, and <u>VLAN ID translation **is** supported</u>.

Only frames with specified C-VID map to the EVC.

C-VID does not have to match.
(C-VID translation **is** supported.)

If UNI-to-EVC connectivity is **port-based**, <u>VLAN ID translation **is not** supported</u>.

All frames map to the EVC.

Caution: *The terms **port-based**, **one-channel**, and **multi-channel** are not MEF terms. They are used informally in this book to convey concepts a little more directly and simply than proper MEF terminology allows. In MEF specifications, these three forms of connectivity emerge from the definition of service attributes (**All-to-One Bundling**, **Bundling**, **CE-VLAN ID / EVC Map** and **CE-VLAN ID Preservation**) and requirements for their configuration.*

4.4
Carrier Ethernet Services

In this section:

The MEF defines one Carrier Ethernet service type for each type of EVC:

- **E-Line** service type based on the **point-to-point** EVC

- **E-LAN** service type based on the **multipoint-to-multipoint** EVC

- **E-Tree** service type based on the **rooted-multipoint** EVC

For each Carrier Ethernet **service type** (E-Line, E-LAN, and E-Tree), the MEF defines two services:

- A *port-based*, or *private*, service

- A *VLAN-based*, or *virtual private*, service

This results in six Carrier Ethernet services, as shown in the following table.

Service Type (EVC)	Carrier Ethernet Service	
	Port-Based	VLAN-Based
E-Line (point-to-point)	EPL (Ethernet Private Line)	EVPL (Ethernet Virtual Private Line)
E-LAN (multipoint-to-multipoint)	EP-LAN (Ethernet Private LAN)	EVP-LAN (Ethernet Virtual Private LAN)
E-Tree (rooted multipoint)	EP-Tree (Ethernet Private Tree)	EVP-Tree (Ethernet Virtual Private Tree)

Port-based (private) services cannot be service multiplexed. At each UNI, all service frames map to the EVC.

VLAN-based (virtual private) services can be service multiplexed. At each UNI, service frames map to EVCs based on VLAN ID.

Note: *In addition to these complete (UNI-to-UNI) services, the MEF defines two types of E-Access services (Access EPL and Access EVPL), which are described later in this chapter.*

Related Links

Service Multiplexing on p. 76
E-Access Services on p. 87

4.4.1
Nine Kinds of Service Connectivity

Together, the three types of EVCs (point-to-point, multipoint-to-multipoint, or rooted-multipoint) combine with the three forms of UNI-to-EVC connectivity (port-based, one-channel, or multi-channel) to produce nine kinds of service connectivity.

The following table lists the nine kinds of connectivity, along with proper MEF terminology for each.

	EVC Type	UNI-to-EVC Connectivity (Informal Terminology Not Sanctioned by the MEF)	MEF Service Terminology (For Reference)		Key Attribute Values	
			Service Type	Service Name	All-to-One Bundling	Bundling
1	Point-to-point	Port-based	E-Line	EPL	Enabled	Disabled
2		One-channel		EVPL	Disabled	Enabled/ Disabled*
3		Multi-channel		EVPL	Disabled	Enabled
4	Multipoint-to-multipoint	Port-based	E-LAN	EP-LAN	Enabled	Disabled
5		One-channel		EVP-LAN	Disabled	Enabled/ Disabled*
6		Multi-channel		EVP-LAN	Disabled	Enabled
7	Rooted-multipoint	Port-based	E-Tree	EP-Tree	Enabled	Disabled
8		One-channel		EVP-Tree	Disabled	Enabled/ Disabled*
9		Multi-channel		EVP-Tree	Disabled	Enabled

* For one-channel connectivity, Bundling can be Enabled or Disabled. However, only one CE-VLAN ID can map to the EVC.

Caution: *The terms* **port-based**, **one-channel**, *and* **multi-channel** *are not MEF terms. They are used informally in this book to convey concepts a little more directly and simply than proper MEF terminology allows. In MEF specifications, these three forms of connectivity emerge from the definition of service attributes (**All-to-One Bundling**, **Bundling**, **CE-VLAN ID / EVC Map** and **CE-VLAN ID Preservation**) and requirements for their configuration.*

4.4.2
Three Forms of E-Line Service

In the following figure, E-Line services are classified into three varieties (**Port-Based**, **One-Channel**, and **Multi-Channel**) based in how Ethernet frames map to the EVC at UNIs.

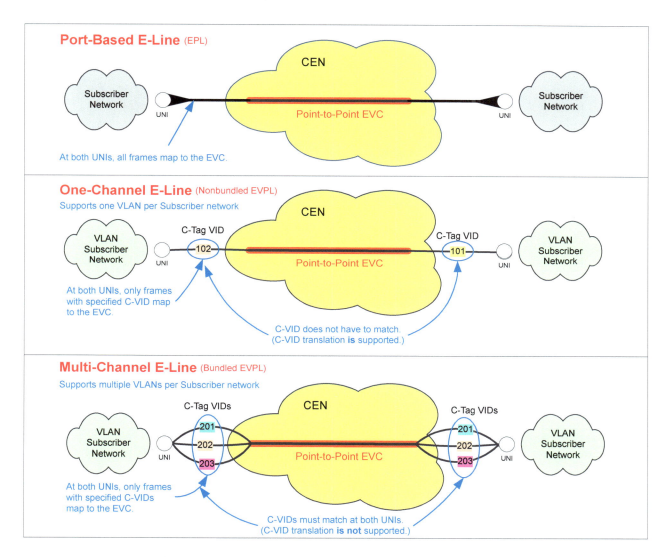

 Important: *This system of classification aligns with MEF service specifications, but is not sanctioned by the MEF. It was created for this book to help explain E-Line services conceptually.*

The One-Channel E-Line service supports C-Tag VID translation. The other two varieties of E-Line service do not support C-Tag VID translation.

4.4.3
Three Forms of E-LAN Service

In the following figure, E-LAN services are classified into three varieties (**Port-Based**, **One-Channel**, and **Multi-Channel**) based in how Ethernet frames map to the EVC at UNIs.

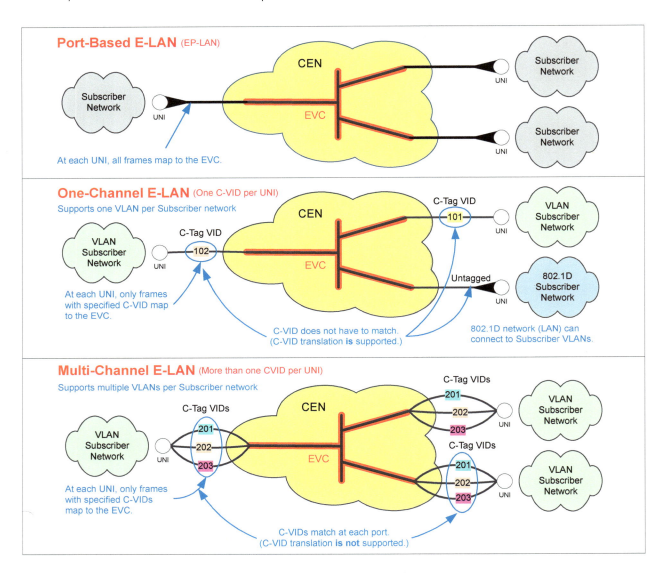

 Important: *This system of classification aligns with MEF service specifications, but is not sanctioned by the MEF. It was created for this book to help explain E-LAN services conceptually.*

The One-Channel E-LAN supports C-Tag VID translation. The other two varieties of E-LAN service do not support C-Tag VID translation.

4.5

Traffic Management and OAM

In this section:

4.5.1

Bandwidth Profiles

Bandwidth profiles are used in Carrier Ethernet services to quantify the amount of traffic that a service supports. They are needed because Carrier Ethernet services are defined at Layer 2, rather than at Layer 1.

Traditional TDM-based Telecom services (defined at Layer 1) do not use bandwidth profiles because their bandwidth is easily defined and understood by one number: the bit rate of the associated TDM circuit. Carrier Ethernet services, in contrast, do not offer Layer 1 bandwidth directly to customers. Instead, they support Layer 2 bandwidth, as required, up to agreed limits that are specified in the service agreement using bandwidth profiles. These limits are specified for two purposes:

• To ensure that traffic (up to agreed limits) is allowed into the CEN and is properly treated

• To protect the service provider from excess traffic in the CEN

Sizing a Layer 2 service using bandwidth profiles involves more than sizing a Layer 1 service:

• Bandwidth profiles quantify traffic bursts (not just steady traffic).

• Bandwidth profiles quantify two types of traffic: committed traffic (green) and excess traffic (yellow).

A bandwidth profile consists of six parameter values that govern operation of a **bandwidth profile algorithm** that processes service frames at a reference point (typically, at a UNI).

Bandwidth Profile Parameter		Units of Measure or Values
CIR	Committed Information Rate	Bits per second
CBS	Committed Burst Size	Bytes
EIR	Excess Information Rate	Bits per second
EBS	Excess Burst Size	Bytes
CF	Coupling Flag	N or Y
CM	Color Mode	color-blind or color-aware

Details of bandwidth profile processing are beyond the scope of this book, but the process assigns each service frame to one of three categories of compliance:

- **Green** (CIR-conformant) — Service frames are in-profile with respect to service performance objectives and are forwarded.

- **Yellow** (EIR-conformant) — Service frames are out-of-profile with respect to service performance objectives, but are still forwarded (with discard-eligible status)

- **Red** (Non-conformant) — Service frames are out-of-profile and immediately discarded

The following figure shows bandwidth profile functionality decomposed into two parts:

- **Compliance monitoring functionality** — The "Bandwidth Profiler" marks service frames red, yellow, or green as they pass by.

- **Policing functionality** — The policer stops and discards service frames marked red (non-compliant), preventing their delivery.

Reproduced with permission of the Metro Ethernet Forum

Although green frames and yellow frames both pass the policer, service performance objectives only apply to green frames. Yellow frames are consequently more likely to be dropped or delayed, compared to green frames.

In MEF service definitions, bandwidth profiles apply at UNIs. Because service frames travel in two directions at every UNI (ingress and egress), bandwidth profiles can be assigned in two directions:

- **Ingress bandwidth profile** — A bandwidth profile applied to service frames entering the CEN from the CE

- **Egress bandwidth profile** — A bandwidth profile applied to service frames exiting the CEN to the CE

4.5.2
Quality of Service (QoS)

Quality of service (QoS) refers to performance objectives specified, per MEF standards, in the service agreement.

Class of Service (CoS)

Recognizing that different types of traffic have different QoS requirements, the MEF defines a framework that allows service providers to offer more than one QoS option. In this framework, the service provider defines a small number of QoS options, each called a **Class of Service (CoS)**. Each service frame is assigned to a CoS upon ingress to the CEN[36], and that assignment determines the frame's QoS treatment thereafter within the CEN.

This system allows traffic from different services to mix in the network (each frame is delivered according to its assigned CoS). It also allows different frames within the same service to be assigned different QoS treatment.

Performance Specification

QoS for each class of service CoS is specified, per MEF standards, using five performance attributes:

1. **Availability**–The percentage of time that a service is useable
2. **Resiliency**–The service's ability to continue to perform under fault conditions
3. **Frame Loss Ratio**–The number of service frames lost as a percentage of those sent
4. **Frame Delay**–The time a service frame spends in transit
5. **Inter-Frame Delay Variation**–The variation in the delays experienced by different service frames

Performance specification is key to defining Carrier Ethernet services in the abstract, apart from implementation (measurable qualities of the service are defined without defining how those qualities are achieved).

4.5.3
Operations, Administration and Management (OAM)

Carrier Ethernet services include Operations, Administration and Management (OAM) support at two levels:

- **Link OAM (LOAM)**–Provides OAM functionality across individual Ethernet links, such as UNIs.

- **Service OAM (SOAM)**–Provides per-service OAM functionality, end-to-end, across the network and distributes that functionality between administrative organizations (subscribers, service providers, and operators)

SOAM functionality is used for two purposes:

- **Performance Management (PM)**–To measure things like frame loss and frame delay that, in turn, are used to calculate performance metrics that, in turn, are used to verify that performance objectives specified in the service agreement are met

- **Connectivity Fault Management (CFM)**–To continuously monitor service connectivity, to detect faults, to raise alarms, and to help network operators troubleshoot connectivity issues when they arise

---

36 CoS can be assigned to service frames in several ways. For example, all frames within a service can be assigned to the same CoS. Alternatively, CoS can be assigned to individual frames, based on values encoded within the frames themselves (by the subscriber), such as the value of the PCP bits in the C-Tag, or the value of the differentiated services code point (DSCP) in the IP header.

4.6
Carrier Ethernet Services Over Multiple Carrier Networks

In this section:

Up to this point, for simplicity, we have assumed that services can be implemented over one carrier network. But many customers need to connect sites that are not all reachable through a single carrier network.

4.6.1
General Reference Model

The MEF extends the basic reference model to define Carrier Ethernet services across multiple networks called Operator CENs[37]. Each Operator CEN is understood to be independently owned and operated.

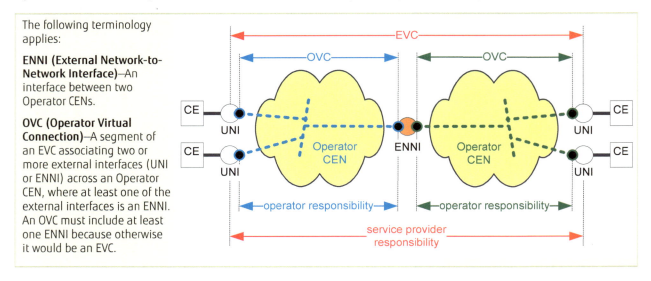

The following terminology applies:

ENNI (External Network-to-Network Interface)—An interface between two Operator CENs.

OVC (Operator Virtual Connection)—A segment of an EVC associating two or more external interfaces (UNI or ENNI) across an Operator CEN, where at least one of the external interfaces is an ENNI. An OVC must include at least one ENNI because otherwise it would be an EVC.

There is still only one service provider who is responsible to the subscriber for the service as a whole, the service is still implemented with exactly one EVC, and the basic reference model remains unchanged (sufficient to define the service from the subscriber's perspective).

The general reference model is used to divide an EVC into segments (OVCs) with well-defined handoff at ENNIs. Network operators then independently implement OVCs such that their concatenation across the aggregate network produces the required EVC.

---

37   Early MEF specifications use the term MEN (Metro Ethernet Network) in place of CEN. CEN and MEN mean the same thing.

OVCs, like EVCs, can be point-to-point, multipoint-to-multipoint, or rooted-multipoint.

This example includes one multipoint-to-multipoint OVC and two point-to-point OVCs.

An **OVC End Point** associates an OVC with a specific external interface (UNI or ENNI). The OVC end point is not the UNI or ENNI. UNIs and ENNIs are not OVC end points.

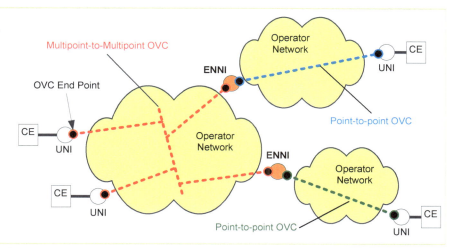

Related Links

Basic Reference Model on p. 72

4.6.2
E-Access Services

Generally, the MEF leaves it up to the service provider and operators to work out the details of OVC-based services as required (following MEF standards, of course). But, because Ethernet access applications are very common, the MEF goes one step further: to define E-Access services (industry-standard OVC-based Ethernet services for Ethernet access applications).

An E-Access service is an OVC-based Ethernet service that allows a service provider to reach out-of-franchise subscriber locations.

The business model has two principle stakeholders:

- **Ethernet Access Provider**–The organization that operates the access network and offers the E-Access service to the service provider

- **Service Provider**–The organization that commissions the E-Access service from the access provider

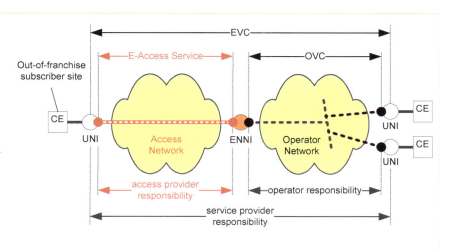

The service provider commissions E-Access services to support end-to-end (UNI-to-UNI) subscriber services, but the E-Access services are decoupled from (independent of) the end-to-end services they support. The MEF defines two E-Access services: the **Access EPL** (a port-based point-to-point E-Access service) and the **Access EVPL** (a VLAN-based point-to-point E-Access service). Both are point-to-point, OVC-based, UNI-to-ENNI Ethernet connections.

4.6.3
Carrier Ethernet Service Over Multiple Networks

In the multi-network service framework the CEN is replaced by two or more of **Operator CENs** interconnected by **ENNIs** (External Network-to-Network Interfaces).

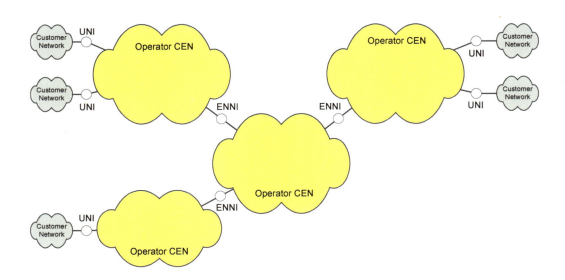

The Carrier Ethernet service does not change from the subscriber's perspective. There is still only one service provider who is responsible to the subscriber for the service as a whole, and the service is still defined with exactly one EVC. For example, the service may be an EVP-LAN supporting three customer VLAN IDs as shown in the following figure.

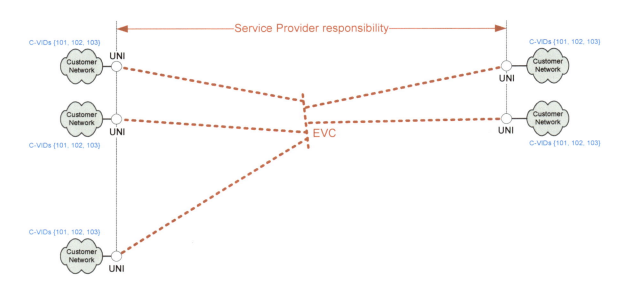

However, to collaboratively implement the service, the EVC is decomposed into OVCs, which are assigned to Operator CENs such that the concatenation of OVCs across the aggregate network produces the required EVC.

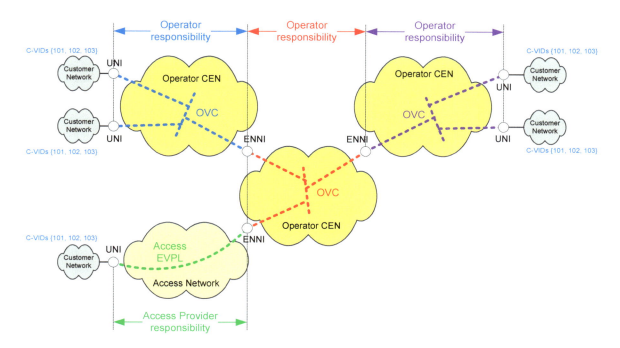

Although nothing changes from the subscriber's perspective, the service provider now has a business relationship with each Operator (akin to a general contractor's relationships with a subcontractor). OVC-based **Operator Services** are defined, and the service provider purchases those services from Operators. Operator services are similar to EVC-based (E-Line, E-LAN, and E-Tree) services in that they are defined abstractly (by specifying interfaces and service behavior with respect to those interfaces). However, Operator services include ENNI interfaces (not just UNIs).

Well-defined service handoff at ENNIs is key to this decomposition.

4.6.4
Service Handoff at ENNIs

An ENNI is a high-bandwidth interface between two Operator CENs that can be used to support numerous Carrier Ethernet services.

When one Operator CEN hands off an Ethernet frame to another Operator CEN, the handoff must include more than just the original service frame that was transmitted across the UNI from the customer/subscriber at service ingress. The following service-related information about the frame must also be relayed:

- Information to identify the frame to a particular service

- Information to identify QoS (quality of service) treatment that the frame should receive

- Information to identify the frame's color (green / yellow), indicating service commitment (drop-eligibility)

MEF standards adopt the service VLAN tag (S-Tag) defined in IEEE 802.1Q (2011) to address this issue.

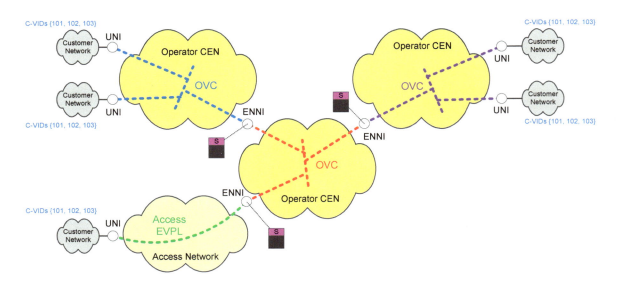

The MEF requires service frames to be S-Tagged <u>at ENNIs only</u> (not within the Operator CENs themselves). Use of S-Tags within an Operator CEN is discretionary (not required, not disallowed).

The S-Tag

Double-Tagged Ethernet frame

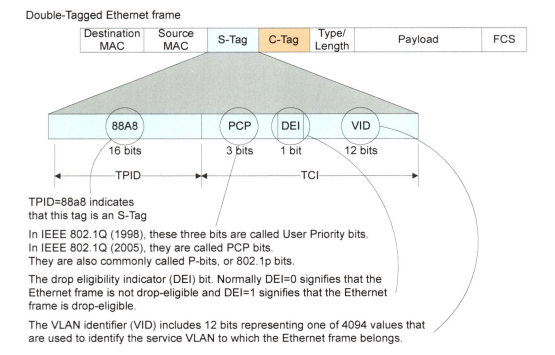

TPID=88a8 indicates that this tag is an S-Tag

In IEEE 802.1Q (1998), these three bits are called User Priority bits.
In IEEE 802.1Q (2005), they are called PCP bits.
They are also commonly called P-bits, or 802.1p bits.

The drop eligibility indicator (DEI) bit. Normally DEI=0 signifies that the Ethernet frame is not drop-eligible and DEI=1 signifies that the Ethernet frame is drop-eligible.

The VLAN identifier (VID) includes 12 bits representing one of 4094 values that are used to identify the service VLAN to which the Ethernet frame belongs.

Note: *The 12-bit VID field allows 4096 values, but only 4094 values can be used for VLAN identification because VID values 0 and FFF are reserved for other uses.*

The following information is encoded in the S-Tag at ENNIs:

- **OVC End Point Identification** — Ingress ENNI frames are mapped to OVC end points based on S-VLAN ID value.

- **CoS identification** — Ingress ENNI frames are mapped to CoS based on S-Tag PCP value.

- **Color identification**—Color (green/yellow drop-eligibility) can be assigned to an ingress ENNI frame in either one of two ways: based on S-Tag DEI bit value, or based on S-Tag PCP value.

4.6.5
Hairpin Switching at ENNIs

Hairpin Switching—When an Ethernet frame is forwarded from the same interface that it was received on.

MEF standards allow hairpin switching at ENNIs to support applications such as the following:

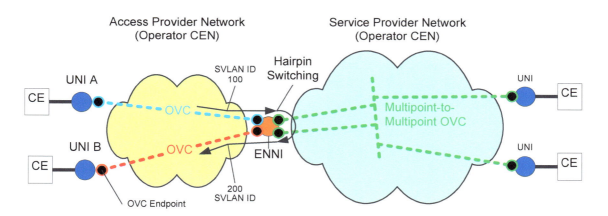

In this example, the subscriber requires an EP-LAN or EVP-LAN service between four sites (UNIs), two of which are outside of the service provider network. To reach these sites, the service provider has purchased two E-Access services (point-to-point OVCs) from an access provider, both terminating at the same ENNI.

The service provider supports bridging between UNI A and UNI B through hairpin switching behavior, which occurs within the service provider network as follows: a service frame received from the access network through the ENNI is forwarded back through the same ENNI with a change of S-VLAN ID so that it associates to a different OVC when it returns to the access network.

To the access network, hairpin switching functions like a remote bridging service. An access network with only point-to-point service capability can provide EP-LAN or EVP-LAN services to customers by partnering with a service provider that supplies bridging functionality through hairpin switching.

4.7
Summary

You should now understand Carrier Ethernet well enough to begin specialized follow-on training to pass the MEF-CECP Exam, if that is your goal. In particular, you should have a basic understanding of Ethernet as it is used in Enterprise networking, a conceptual understanding of networking technology leading up to and motivating Carrier Ethernet, and a high-level understanding of Carrier Ethernet service definitions and terminology.

Most MEF-CECP exam questions are about Carrier Ethernet service standards and requirements, but the exam also tests general knowledge about Carrier Ethernet service applications and about the strengths and limitations of technologies that can be used to implement Carrier Ethernet services.

Where To Go From Here

The following information was current when this book was published. For the latest information about Fujitsu's vendor-neutral MEF-CECP training options, refer to www.fujitsu.com/us/products/network/training/ethernet-training/.

Fujitsu Instructor-Led Training — If you prefer face-to-face training, you can get it from Fujitsu. Fujitsu's MEF-CECP Exam training course uses Fujitsu's study guide and training app and is led by an MEF-CECP certified instructor. Fujitsu's training course is MEF-accredited and culminates with options to take the exam, proctored by the instructor. The course is offered regularly at Fujitsu's Richardson, Texas campus and is available at other locations by request. For more information, email Ed.svcs@fnc.fujitsu.com.

Fujitsu *MEF-CECP Study Guide* — Fujitsu's popular MEF-CECP study guide, now in its third edition, has helped numerous people pass the MEF-CECP exam. Many have passed the exam studying the book alone. Others have used the book in combination with Fujitsu's Exam Trainer app and/or to prepare for an MEF-CECP training course. The third edition of this study guide has been updated to align with MEF-CECP Certification Blueprint C. Like previous editions, this edition is designed for two purposes: to help you prepare for the MEF-CECP exam and to serve a practical general reference book explaining MEF-defined Carrier Ethernet concepts and standards. The guide features careful explanations, numerous custom color graphics, and more than 200 practice questions with answers. The study guide assumes that you have a basic understanding of Ethernet, but no prior knowledge of Carrier Ethernet. The guide covers all topics that are included in the MEF-CECP exam (specified by Blueprint C). Material is presented systematically, beginning with MEF service definitions (the core content that accounts for most exam questions) and building outward. Each lesson ends with a set of multiple-choice review questions similar to those appearing in the MEF-CECP exam. The study guide is available from Amazon.com in print and Kindle formats.

Fujitsu MEF-CECP Exam Trainer App — If you want to practice using questions that are similar to those on the real exam, this mobile app is ideal. The Exam Trainer app offers more than 200 multiple-choice practice questions (from the study guide) in several study modes and provides feedback. The Exam Trainer emphasizes learning over memorization by randomizing the sequence of both questions and answers. Got a question wrong? The app provides a brief explanation or pointer to study guide content. You can even record your scores to see how they improve over time. This app has been updated for MEF-CECP Exam Blueprint C and is available for iPhone, iPad, Android, and Windows 8 devices.

A
Reference Details

In this appendix:

Praise for Fujitsu's MEF-CECP Study Guide (From Amazon reviews)

"I purchased the book two weeks before the exam. The book was a great help for passing the exam. I had no prior experiences with the MEF specifications. The book provides an excellent overview of architecture framework, service definitions and service attributes, among other topics. I spent over 20 hours on this study guide, and passed the exam with a good score."

"The book is extremely precise, thorough, well presented, and well illustrated. It is also very easy to read, understand, and learn from. The end-of-chapter review questions and the in-chapter "test your understanding" questions and answers are challenging tools that effectively instill a deep grasp of the material."

"Ordered this book (and the Kindle edition for a few dollars additional) 10 days prior to going to a company sponsored boot camp. I am glad I did. Boot camps are great but for the MEF exam you need to learn dozens of acronyms, service definitions, and attributes specific to Carrier Ethernet. This material gave me the head start I needed."

"After reading this book I passed my CECP the first time. I recommend reading the book cover to cover and re-read if you don't have a complete understanding. Take the knowledge check at the end of the chapter and if you're able to score 90% and up on the first try you'll pass the test. You can get Fujitsu Exam Trainer app and take the simulated exam for more help."

1st Edition: (July 2012)    2nd Edition: (Dec. 2013)    3rd Edition: (Oct. 2015)

The latest edition is available in print and Kindle formats from Amazon.com .

A.1
MAC Addressing in Detail

In this section:

A.1.1   Organizationally Unique Identifier (OUI)
A.1.2   Destination MAC Addresses
A.1.3   Source MAC Addresses
A.1.4   Multicast MAC Addresses

Media access control (MAC) addresses come from a 48-bit address space containing 2^{48} or 281,474,976,710,656 possible MAC addresses.

For human recognition, a MAC address is commonly represented using 6 groups of 2 hexadecimal digits:

MAC address = XX-XX-XX-XX-XX-XX

Where each X represents a hexadecimal digit from the set {0, 1, 2, 3, 4, 5, 6, 7, 8, 9, A, B, C, D, E, F}

In a computer, a MAC address is binary composed of six 8-bit bytes:

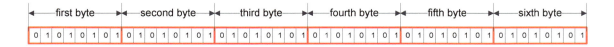

The following figure illustrates conversion of binary
10101010.11110000.11000001.11100010.01110111.01010001 to hexadecimal AA–F0–C1–E2–77–51.

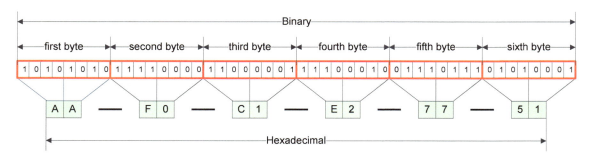

Conversion Table

Binary	Hexadecimal	Binary	Hexadecimal	Binary	Hexadecimal	Binary	Hexadecimal
0000	0	0100	4	1000	8	1100	C
0001	1	0101	5	1001	9	1101	D
0010	2	0110	6	1010	A	1110	E
0011	3	0111	7	1011	B	1111	F

A.1.1
Organizationally Unique Identifier (OUI)

The 48-bit MAC address is divided into two parts:

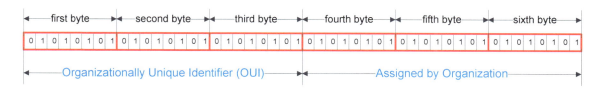

The first 24 bits constitute an Organizationally Unique Identifier (OUI), which indicates the organization (typically an equipment manufacturer) that is responsible for unique assignment of the remaining 24 bits of the MAC address. The second 24 bits are assigned by that organization.

OUIs are issued by the IEEE to organizations that apply for them.

A.1.2
Destination MAC Addresses

The space of destination MAC addresses is divided into three parts, each used for a different purpose:

- **Unicast address**—Targets a single Ethernet interface

- **Multicast address**—Targets a group of interfaces that are provisioned to accept the address

- **Broadcast address**—Targets all Ethernet interfaces in the network

Classification is largely based on the value of the most significant bit (the right-most bit) of the first byte.

If that bit is 0, the address is unicast.

If that bit is 1, the address is multicast or broadcast.

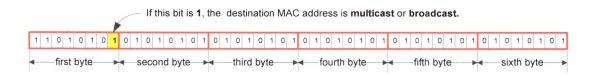

If all bits are 1, the address is broadcast.

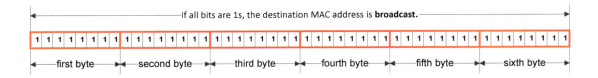

In hexadecimal, classification is determined by the second digit. Consider an arbitrary MAC address:

> MAC address =xY-xx-xx-xx-xx-xx
>
> Where each x and **Y** represents a hexadecimal digit from the set {0, 1, 2, 3, 4, 5, 6, 7, 8, 9, A, B, C, D, E, F}

If the second digit (Y) is even (0, 2, 4, 6, 8, A, C, or E), the address is unicast.

If the second digit (Y) is odd (1, 3, 5, 7, 9, B, D, or F), the address is multicast or broadcast.

If all digits are F, the address is broadcast.

Note: *There is only one broadcast address. In hexadecimal, the broadcast address is FF-FF-FF-FF-FF-FF.*

A.1.3
Source MAC Addresses

The space of source MAC addresses is identical to the space of unicast destination MAC addresses.

In binary, the most significant bit (the right-most bit) of the first byte is 0.

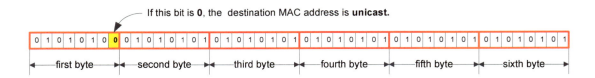

In hexadecimal, the second digit (**Y**) in the MAC address (xY-xx-xx-xx-xx-xx) is even (0, 2, 4, 6, 8, A, C, or E).

For a given Ethernet interface, the following three MAC addresses match:

* Factory-assigned MAC address of the interface

* Source MAC address of any Ethernet frame sent <u>from</u> the interface

* Destination MAC address of any <u>unicast</u> Ethernet frame sent <u>to</u> the interface

A.1.4
Multicast MAC Addresses

A multicast MAC address is a type of destination MAC address that targets all of the Ethernet interfaces in the network that have been provisioned to accept it.

In binary, a MAC address is multicast if it contains at least one 0 and the most significant bit (the right-most bit) of the first byte is 1.[38]

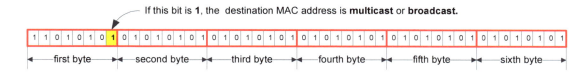

In hexadecimal, a MAC address (X**X**-XX-XX-XX-XX-XX) is multicast if its second digit is odd (1, 3, 5, 7, 9, B, D, or F) and not all digits are F.

Multicast addresses are typically used by higher-layer protocols or applications running on a subset of network devices. Multicasting is perfectly suited to the situation where all currently active instances of a protocol have to communicate with each other without knowing individual addresses or even knowing how many other instances of the protocol are active in the network. Multicasting allows devices running the protocol to communicate without burdening devices that are not currently running the protocol. When a protocol is instantiated on a device, the Ethernet interface is configured to accept the multicast address(es) associated with the protocol. Until then, the interface can ignore that traffic.

The following table lists a few examples.

Example Multicast Address	Usage
01-80-C2-00-00-00	Spanning Tree Protocols (for bridges) IEEE 802.1D (includes STP, RSTP, and MSTP)
01-80-C2-00-00-01	PAUSE (IEEE 802.3)
01-80-C2-00-00-02	Link OAM and LACP/LAMP (IEEE 802.3)
01-80-C2-00-00-03	Port Authentication (IEEE 801.1X)
01-80-C2-00-00-07	E-LMI (MEF 16)
01-80-C2-00-00-08	Spanning Tree Protocols (for provider bridges) IEEE 802.1AD
01-80-C2-00-00-0E	LLDP (IEEE 802.1AB)
01-80-C2-00-00-20 through 01-80-C2-00-00-2F	GARP (IEEE 802.1Q), MRP (IEEE 802.1ak), Block

---

38 If all bits are 1, the MAC address is the broadcast MAC address. In hexadecimal the broadcast address is FF-FF-FF-FF-FF-FF.

A.2
VLAN Bridging In Detail

In this section:

A.2.1   VLAN Identifiers
A.2.2   VLAN Port Association
A.2.3   Edge Ports and Network Ports
A.2.4   Mapping Ingress Frames to VLANs at Edge Ports

A.2.5   VLAN Tagging and Frame Forwarding
A.2.6   Priority-Tagged Ethernet Frames
A.2.7   About IEEE 802.1Q and VLAN Bridging Terminology

To emulate IEEE 802.1D MAC bridging within each VLAN, VLAN-aware bridges/switches are configured to perform MAC learning on a per-VLAN basis and to forward frames on a per-VLAN basis.

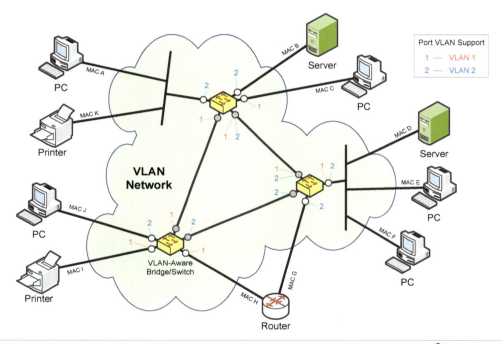

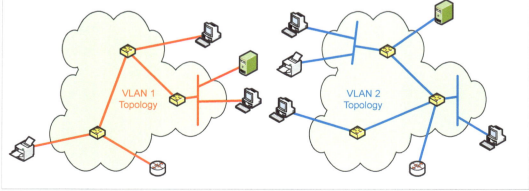

Typically, each Ethernet end station is assigned to one (and only one) VLAN, as shown in the previous figure. However, Ethernet end stations that are <u>VLAN-aware</u> (not typical) can be assigned to more than one VLAN.

Note: *For simplicity, this book assumes that Ethernet end stations are <u>not</u> VLAN-aware.*

Each VLAN-aware bridge/switch is configured to:

- Associate a specific set of ports with each VLAN

- Map each received frame[39] onto a single VLAN and forward it appropriately, <u>using MAC learning and forwarding, constrained to that VLAN</u>

A.2.1
VLAN Identifiers

Each VLAN-aware bridge/switch supports up to 4094 VLANs. Each bridge/switch identifies VLANs internally (within itself) using an internal VLAN identifier (VID) that takes a value from the set 1...4094. A tagged Ethernet frame also includes a VLAN identifier (VID) that also takes a value from the set 1...4094. For clarity, the following notation is used in this book to distinguish between the two (when necessary):

- **Bridge_VID**—Denotes the value of a VLAN identifier (1...4094) internal to a bridge/switch

- **Tag_VID**—Denotes the value of a VLAN identifier (1...4094) in a tagged Ethernet frame

For simplicity, a VLAN can be implemented in the network using a single value (say 1776) for all `Bridge_VIDs` and `Tag_VIDs` associated with the VLAN. However, this is not required. A VLAN can be implemented using a different value of `Bridge_VID` at each bridge/switch and (yet other) different values of `Tag_VID` to identify Ethernet frames in each link between bridge/switch ports. Thus, implementation of a network VLAN can involve many VLAN identifiers with values that can match (for simplicity), but do not have to match (for flexibility).

A.2.2
VLAN Port Association

Each VLAN-aware bridge/switch is configured to associate a specific set of ports with each VLAN it supports.

Assignments shown in the following figure support the two loop-free VLAN topologies previously shown.

---

[39] Excluding non-traffic bearing Ethernet frames, such as Layer 2 Control Protocol (L2CP) frames, which are not always mapped to VLANs.

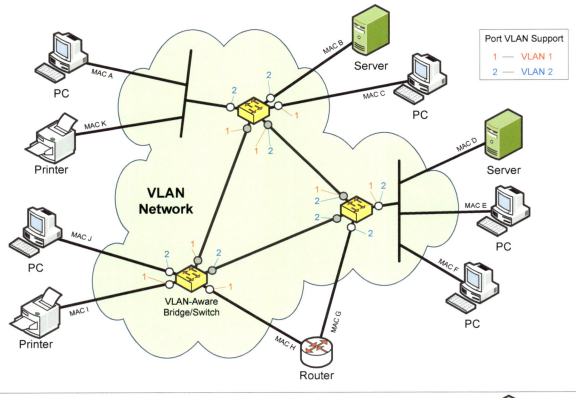

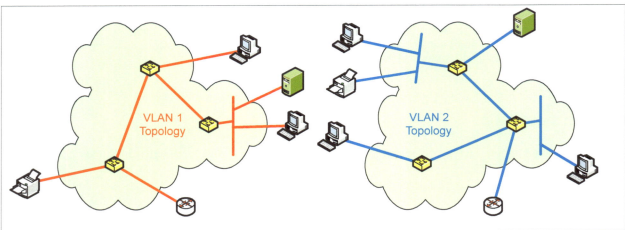

This solves part of the problem: <u>If the VLAN of an ingress frame is known</u>[40], the bridge/switch knows how to forward it (using MAC learning and forwarding, constrained to the ports that have been identified with the VLAN).[41]

---

40 The term **ingress** means incoming or received. The term **egress** means outgoing or transmitted.
41 An VLAN-aware bridge/switch keeps a separate forwarding database (or the equivalent) for each VLAN.

But how does the bridge/switch know which VLAN an incoming frame belongs to? After all, each port can support many different VLANs, and the standard Ethernet frame (an IEEE 802.1D Ethernet frame) does not include VLAN identification information encoded within it.

A.2.3
Edge Ports and Network Ports

VLAN-aware bridges/switches support two types of ports:

- **Edge Port** — A port that supports (non-VLAN-aware[42]) Ethernet end stations is an **edge port** with respect to the VLAN network.

- **Network Port**—A port that connects to another VLAN-aware bridge/switch is a **network port** with respect to the VLAN network.

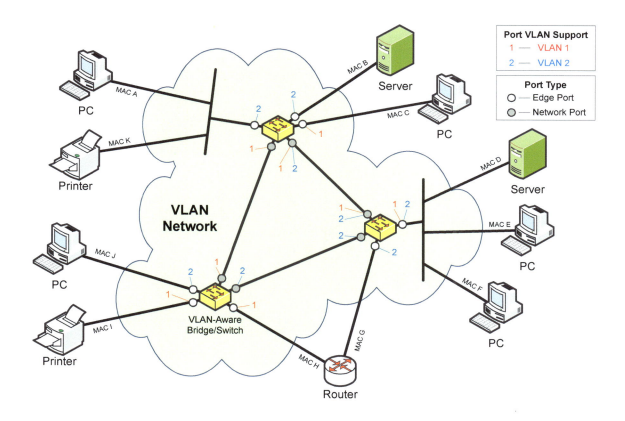

VLAN-aware bridges/switches use two systems to map ingress Ethernet frames to VLANs. One system is used at edge ports and the other system is used at network ports.

---

42 For simplicity, this book assumes that Ethernet end stations are <u>not</u> VLAN-aware (which is typical).

A.2.4
Mapping Ingress Frames to VLANs at Edge Ports

Ethernet frames received at edge ports are standard Ethernet frames, conforming to IEEE 802.1D.

There are two mechanisms for mapping ingress frames to VLANs at edge ports:

- **Per-end-station mapping**—Through provisioning, an edge port can be configured to recognise Ethernet frames sent from an individual subtending Ethernet end station and assign those frames to a VLAN. The *source MAC address* in the Ethernet frame (the MAC address of the sending Ethernet end station) is used for identification.

- **Port-based mapping**—Ingress frames that are not assigned to a VLAN by per-end-station mapping are assigned to the edge port's default VLAN, which is identified by the port's provisioned value of port VLAN identifier (PVID).

PVID (Port VLAN Identifier)—A port configuration attribute whose value (in the range 1 to 4094) declares the VLAN to which ingress frames are assigned by default. The value of PVID is set to match the value of `Bridge_VID` for the VLAN to which frames are to be mapped by default.

Each port can be assigned a different value of PVID (any value in the range 1 to 4094).

The default value of PVID for all ports is 1.

Note: Additionally, so-called priority-tagged frames (described later in this book) are mapped to the PVID VLAN.

Per-end-station mapping and port-based mapping can be applied individually or together at edge ports and on a per-port basis.

In this way, each frame is mapped to a specific VLAN at edge-port ingress. But, that association is known only locally (at one VLAN-aware bridge/switch). So, before a frame is forwarded to another VLAN-aware bridge/switch, a VLAN tag is added to the Ethernet frame to capture the VLAN association for future use by the next bridge/ switch.

Related Links

Priority-Tagged Ethernet Frames on p. 103

A.2.5
VLAN Tagging and Frame Forwarding

All traffic-bearing[43] Ethernet frames passed between VLAN-aware bridges/switches include a VLAN tag that carries VLAN identification information (and some other information, as will be explained).

---

43 Non-traffic bearing frames, such as Layer 2 Control Protocol (L2CP) frames, may not include a VLAN tag.

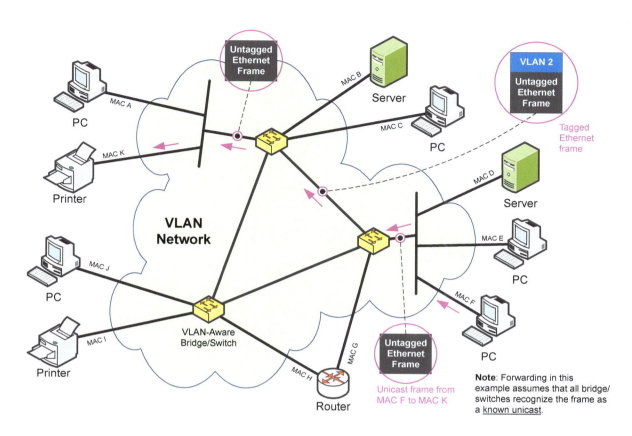

When a VLAN-aware bridge/switch receives an Ethernet frame on an edge port, it associates the frame to a particular VLAN (based on edge port configuration) and then forwards the frame (based on IEEE 802.1D MAC learning <u>restricted to ports that are configured to support the VLAN</u>). If the frame is forwarded to a network port, a VLAN tag is added to the Ethernet frame before it is transmitted.

When a VLAN-aware bridge/switch receives an Ethernet frame on a network port, it uses the VLAN tag to associate the frame to a particular VLAN[44] and then forwards the frame (based on IEEE 802.1D MAC learning <u>restricted to ports that are configured to support the VLAN</u>). If the frame is forwarded to an edge port, the VLAN tag is removed from the Ethernet frame before it is transmitted.

A.2.6
Priority-Tagged Ethernet Frames

A priority-tagged frame is a tagged Ethernet frame with VID=0.

Only Ethernet end stations are allowed to transmit priority-tagged frames.

Per IEEE 802.1Q—2005, a VLAN-aware bridge/switch is allowed to receive priority-tagged frames, but cannot transmit them (without first transforming them to an untagged or normally tagged Ethernet frame).

---

44 Through provisioning, a network port can be configured to associate a `Tag_VID` value (`X`) to an `Bridge_VID` value (`Y`). Then when the port receives an ingress frame with `Tag_VID=X`, the bridge/switch assigns that frame to the VLAN identified by `Bridge_VID=Y`.

Priority tagging has one purpose: to allow Ethernet end stations to declare quality of service (QoS) treatment for frames that it transmits into the VLAN network. QoS treatment is declared by setting PCP bits in the VLAN tag. The VID field in the VLAN tag is not needed and is left empty (set to the null, 0) by convention.

When a VLAN-aware bridge/switch receives a priority-tagged frame through an edge port, it does the following:

1. Extracts the PCP bit value from the VLAN tag for later use.

2. Removes the VLAN tag from the frame.

3. Associates the frame to a VLAN using the same rules that are used for untagged frames[45] (which makes sense considering that the frame is untagged at this point).

4. Forwards and processes the frame as it would any untagged frame, except with appropriate QoS treatment (reflecting the PCP bit value extracted from the original priority tag).

A.2.7
About IEEE 802.1Q and VLAN Bridging Terminology

In 2011 the IEEE replaced its VLAN bridging standard, **IEEE 802.1Q–2005**, which includes only basic VLAN bridging, with **IEEE 802.1Q–2011**, which adds more advanced forms of VLAN bridging, including Provider Bridging (PB) and Provider Backbone Bridging (PBB).

Prior to 2011, many people used the term *IEEE 802.1Q Bridging* (with no year qualification) to refer to basic VLAN bridging. That usage is no longer valid. The term *IEEE 802.1Q Bridging* (with no year qualification) now properly means IEEE 802.1Q–2011 bridging, which includes much more than basic VLAN bridging.

This book uses the following terms:

• **VLAN Bridging** – Refers to basic VLAN bridging, per IEEE 802.1Q–2005, as described in this chapter

• **Provider Bridging** – Refers to Provider Bridging, per IEEE 802.1ad

Noncurrent standards (IEEE 802.1Q–2005 and IEEE 802.1ad) are referenced in this book to clearly separate VLAN schemes. IEEE 802.1Q–2011 is the current standard for VLAN bridging (IEEE 802.1Q–2005) as well as for Provider Bridging (IEEE 802.1ad) and Provider Backbone Bridging (IEEE 802.1ah).

Note: *Provider Bridging was first standardized in IEEE 802.1ad, an amendment to IEEE 802.1Q–2005, which now, like IEEE 802.1Q–2005, has been replaced by IEEE 802.1Q–2011.*

Related Links

Virtual LANs on p. 42

---

45 The frame might be mapped to a VLAN based on source MAC address (if the port has been configured to do so). Otherwise, the frame is mapped to the default port VLAN identified by the port's PVID value.

A.3
Ethernet with IP Routing

Chapter 2 explains how Ethernet supports communication between computers within a LAN. Now we look at Ethernet in a larger networking context: when routers are involved in the network.

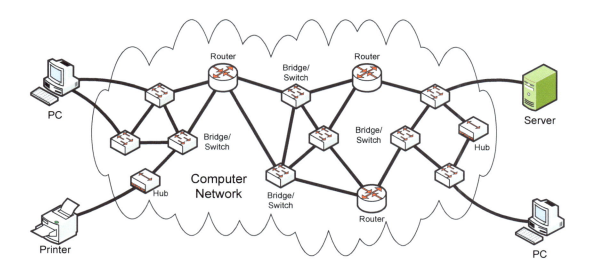

Recall that routers are excluded from Layer 2 Ethernet networks because they are Layer 3 devices.

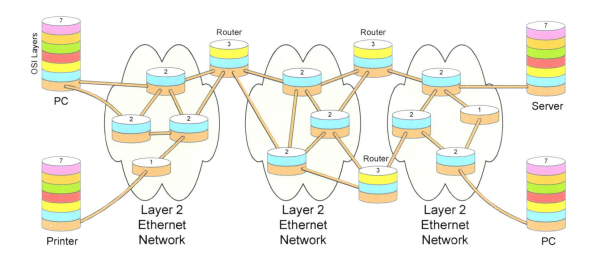

Also recall that each interface to an Ethernet network is an Ethernet end station with a globally unique MAC address.

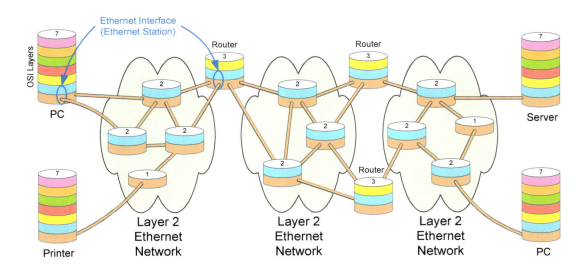

Now consider the following network and suppose that **PC A** needs to communicate with **Server Z**.

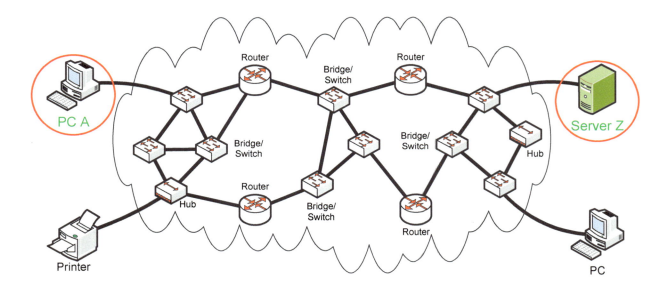

PCA and Server Z cannot communicate through Ethernet alone because they are in different Ethernet networks.

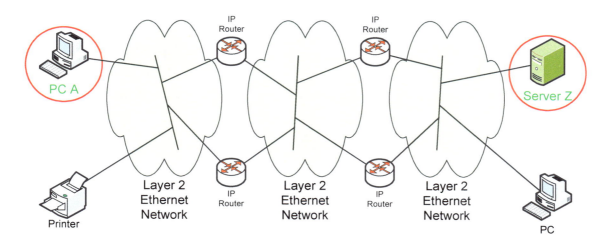

To communicate, PC A creates an IP packet (a Layer 3 PDU) and addresses it (similar to an Ethernet frame) with a source IP address (IP-A, in this example) and a destination IP address (IP-Z, in this example).

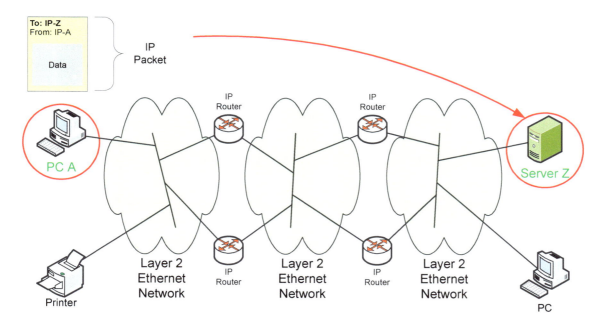

Routers understand IP addresses, but Ethernet networks do not. So PC A places the IP packet in an Ethernet frame and addresses that frame to a router (destination MAC address = MAC B in this example). PC A then transmits the Ethernet frame into the Ethernet network.

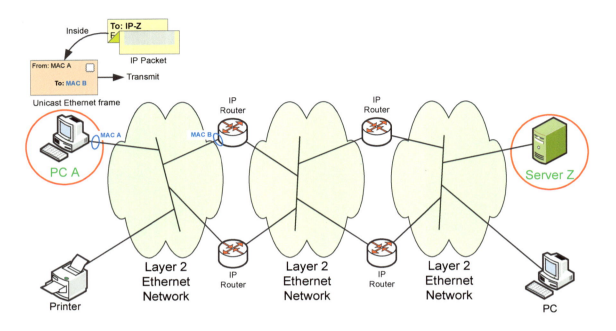

The Ethernet network delivers the Ethernet frame to the router. When the router receives the Ethernet frame, it extracts the IP packet and forgets about the Ethernet frame in which it was delivered. The router then figures out where to send the IP packet next (using IP protocol, which is beyond the scope of this book) and sends it there. In this example the IP packet is placed in a new Ethernet frame, addressed to another router, which can be reached through a different Ethernet network.

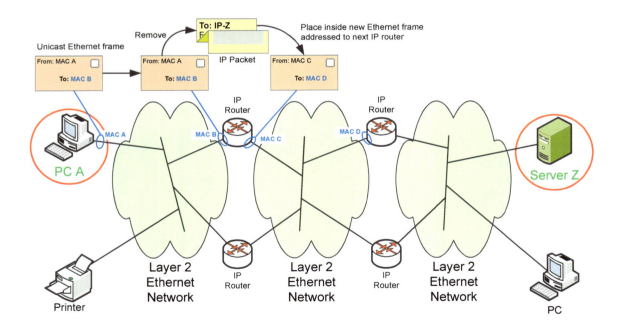

Eventually the IP packet is received by an IP router that shares Ethernet connectivity with Server Z (the IP packet's final destination). That router sends the IP packet to Server Z using Ethernet once again as a vehicle for local delivery.

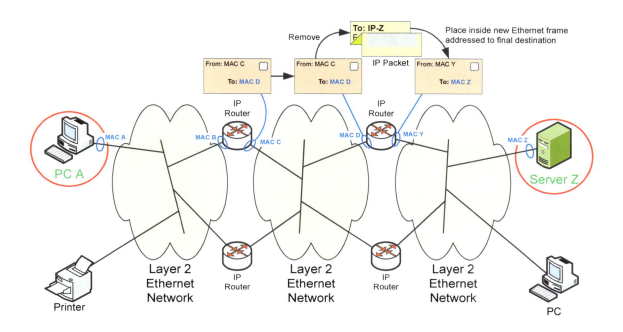

Server Z receives the Ethernet frame, extracts the IP packet and processes it.

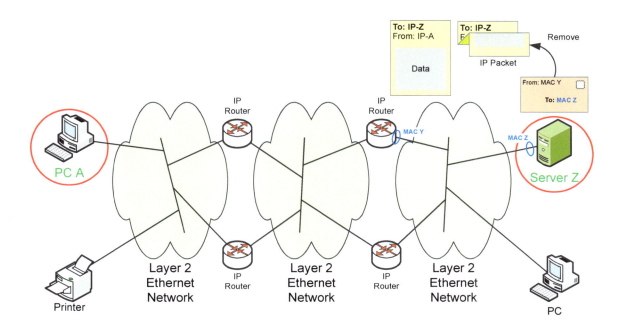

To reply, Server Z creates a new IP packet (addressed to PC A from Server Z), and the process repeats in reverse.

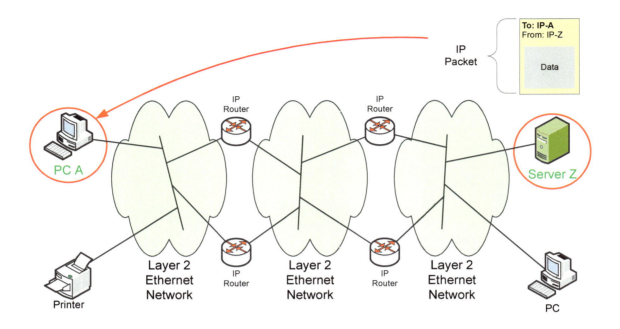

Key observations:

- In this scenario, the two computers cannot communicate through Ethernet alone because they are in different Ethernet networks.

- The two computers communicate through IP packets that remain unchanged during the journey from one computer to the other.

- IP packets are addressed to the final destination, but travel locally through Ethernet networks inside of Ethernet frames that are addressed with MAC addresses.

- Even though MAC addresses are globally unique, they are only locally meaningful. A MAC address has no value outside of the Ethernet network in which the Ethernet end station resides.

Related Links

Ethernet in Local Area Networking on p. 15

A.4
Ethernet over TDM Technologies

In this section:

A.4.1
Ethernet over SONET/SDH (EoS) Technology

Although SONET/SDH technology is designed specifically to support high-quality digital voice circuits for long-distance phone service, it can also support a wide variety of other applications. The SONET/SDH signal payload can be any type of digital signal or data. Most SONET/SDH equipment includes a variety of **access interfaces** to support connection of non-SONET/SDH technologies through the SONET/SDH network. In the following example, two IEEE 802.3 Ethernet interfaces connect through the SONET/SDH network to support an IP access application.

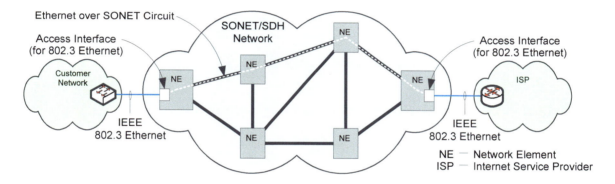

This combination of technologies (Ethernet access interfaces combined with SONET/SDH transport technology) is called **Ethernet over SONET/SDH (EoS)**.

EoS is typically accomplished using GFP (generic framing procedure) protocol at the access interfaces as follows:
1. **At Ingress** – The access interface receives Ethernet frames from the IEEE 802.3 Ethernet link, encapsulates them in a GFP frame, and inserts the GFP frame into the payload of a SONET/SDH signal.
2. **Transport** – A dedicated SONET/SDH circuit, provisioned through the network, transports the Ethernet traffic (as payload within the SONET signal) across the network to the access interface on the other side of the network.
3. **At Egress** – The access interface on the other side of the network removes the GFP frame from the SONET payload, de-encapsulates Ethernet frames from the GFP frame, and transmits the Ethernet frames out the IEEE 802.3 Ethernet link.

From the customer perspective, the EoS service functions very much like a physically cabled Ethernet connection between the two sites. From the carrier perspective, it is basically just another SONET/SDH circuit through the network.

A.4.2
Ethernet over PDH (EoPDH) Technology

Ethernet over PDH (EoPDH) technology is conceptually identical to EoS technology. Two IEEE 802.3 Ethernet interfaces are connected through the PDH network using a PDH circuit with adaptive technology at both ends. The adaptive technology inserts Ethernet frames into the PDH signal payload (at ingress) and extracts Ethernet frames from the PDH signal payload (at egress).

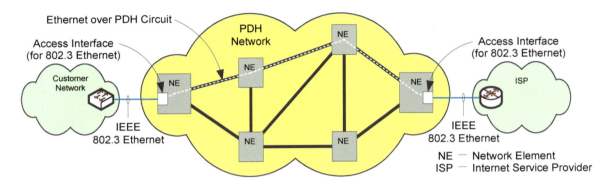

From the customer perspective, an EoPDH service functions very much like a physically cabled Ethernet connection between two sites. From the carrier perspective, it is basically just another PDH circuit through the network.

A.4.3
Ethernet over TDM (EoTDM) Applied for LAN Interconnection

If an EoTDM circuit is applied to interconnect LANs, it behaves (conceptually) very much like a very long Ethernet cable connection.

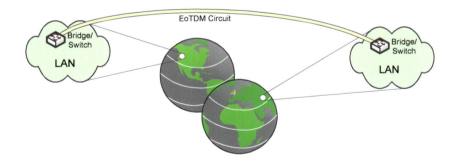

This is ideal from the enterprise network engineering perspective. Distant LANs can be interconnected to form larger aggregate LANs in the same way that nearby LANs are interconnected to form larger aggregate LANs. EoTDM circuits can be used like very long Ethernet cables.

For example, an enterprise with three LAN sites can use two EoTDM circuits to establish an aggregate network with hub-and-spoke topology.

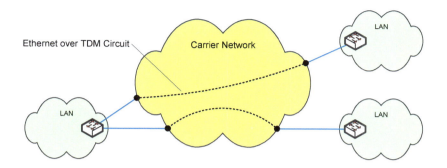

Or, the enterprise can add a third EoTDM circuit to establish full-mesh connectivity.

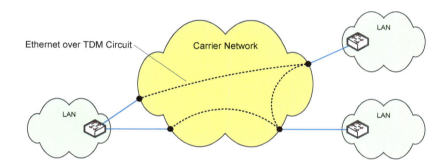

However, there is a catch. EoTDM circuits are services (not Ethernet cables), and they can be expensive compared to packet-based service due to poor bandwidth utilization.

Index

service OAM (SOAM) *85*
service protection *57*
service provider *72*, *86*, *87*
shared media LAN *27*
SOAM (service OAM) *85*
SONET (synchronous optical network) *54*, *56*
source MAC address *24*, *25*, *96*
spanning tree protocols *40*
S-Tag (service VLAN tag) *89*, *90*
start-of-frame delimiter *26*
STM-n (synchronous transport module) signal *54*
storm, broadcast *38*
STP (spanning tree protocol) *40*
subscriber *72*
switch, Ethernet *18*, *36*
switch, hairpin *91*
switch, VLAN-aware *43*
synchronization *57*

T

tag, VLAN *45*
T-Carrier (system of PDH technology) *53*
TCP (transmission control protocol) *22*
TDM (time division multiplexing) *49*
Telecom service *48*
telephone service *49*
time division *49*
time division multiplexing (TDM) *49*
time slot *49*
TPID (tag protocol identifier) *45*, *90*
traffic, drop-eligible *83*
trailer, Ethernet frame *24*
trailer, PDU *17*
translation, VLAN ID *78*
transmission collision *29*
type/length field of Ethernet frame *24*

U

UNI, leaf/root *76*

UNI (user-to-network) interface *72*
unicast, known/unknown *33*
unicast MAC address *25*, *95*
unknown unicast frame *33*
UPSR (unidirectional path-switched ring) protection *58*
UTP (unshielded twisted pair) cable *28*, *31*

V

VID (VLAN identifier) *45*
virtual circuit *66*
virtual LAN (VLAN) *42*
virtual private network (VPN) *12*
VLAN, C-Tag *45*, *90*
VLAN, S-Tag *90*
VLAN (virtual LAN) *42*
VLAN-aware bridge/switch *43*
VLAN-aware bridging *44*, *98*
VLAN-aware Ethernet end station *42*
VLAN-based service *79*
VLAN ID translation *78*
VLAN network *43*
VLAN tag *45*
VLAN topology *44*
VPN (virtual private network) *12*

W

WAN (wide area network) *60*
WAN connectivity *12*, *61*
WDM (wavelength division multiplexing) *92*
WiFi *92*
WiMAX *92*

X

X.25 *67*